The
Empowerment
Church

The Empowerment Church

*Speaking a New Language
for Church Growth*

Carlyle Fielding Stewart III

Abingdon Press
Nashville

THE EMPOWERMENT CHURCH
SPEAKING A NEW LANGUAGE FOR CHURCH GROWTH

Library of Congress Cataloging-in-Publication Data

Stewart, Carlyle Fielding, 1951–
    The empowerment church: speaking a new language for church growth/
Carlyle Fielding Stewart III.
    p. cm.
    Includes bibliographical references (p.).
    ISBN 0-687-06850-9
        1. Church growth—United States.   2. Protestant churches—United
States.   3. African American churches.   I. Title

BR526 .S84 2001
253—dc21   2001018822

01 02 03 04 05 06 07 08 09 10—10 9 8 7 6 5 4 3 2 1

MANUFACTURED IN THE UNITED STATES OF AMERICA

To my wife, Jeane,
and the people
of Hope United
Methodist Church,
with
gratitude
and admiration
for the many ways
you have supported
my ministry to the people of God

I wish to express my
deepest appreciation and
gratitude to my Executive
Administrative Assistant
Jill Day-Foley, whose
painstaking and meticulous
care in typing parts of
the manuscript has
been a blessing.

Contents

Introduction

This book is intended for anyone interested in revitalizing mainline Protestant churches, and underscores the need to develop more *spiritually focused* models of church growth. Based upon more than eighteen years of experience in leading Hope United Methodist Church in Southfield, Michigan, where membership rose from two hundred to more than three thousand members, this book is written for pastors and laypeople who are interested in developing new paradigms for ministry.

The denominational church in general, and black churches in particular, need models of ministry that address the ultimate concerns and needs of the people in the communities in which they are located. Regrettably, some writers, in an effort to be inclusive and to establish greater homogeneity among Christians, have omitted, negated, or dismissed cultural and ethnic needs and aspirations as appropriate foundations for church growth. However, it is precisely those cultural nuances and complexities within various ethnic and racial contexts that must be considered in developing viable church growth models. Jesus understood this and his ministry highlighted the importance of cultural relevance in teaching people. He consistently used parabolic language that reached listeners at the level of their ultimate concerns.

Many black, as well as white, mainstream churches have largely omitted the importance of developing models of ministry that speak to the cultural, spiritual, and relational needs of the American *masses*. On one hand, in an effort to emulate and integrate within white denominations, the resulting *cultural captivity* has prompted numerous black churches to forsake their African roots and fail to develop ministries that are culturally specific to the needs of African Americans. On the other hand, in an attempt to become more mainstream and socially relevant, many white churches have forsaken their evangelical heritage in order to appeal to the liberal compulsions of modern secular society. Thus to their detriment, they have negated their evangelical roots, which gave their early church movements a fervor, vitality, and zeal that enabled them to bring many souls to Christ.

The contributions of whites and blacks to the church, and the positive ways they have influenced the ecclesiastical formations and theological formulations of Christianity in general, is indisputable, but the truth is, there is at present an atrophy, a malaise that is undermining soul-winning efforts of black and white churches in mainline Protestant denominations. This problem is, among other things, largely related to the lack of culturally relevant ministries and the absence of an evangelical spirit of conversion and witness that gives credence, power, and authority to the church and is essential to saving souls.

The mainstream church needs to develop an appreciation and celebration of a variety of cultures and how they have influenced Christianity in all phases of its development. As membership statistics indicate, the devaluation of African culture and heavy reliance on Euro-American values and norms does not appeal to large numbers of African Americans, and may explain why there are fewer of the black underclass in mainstream Protestant denominations. Conversely, the defection of white American mainline Protestantism from its evangelical sources has done very little to appeal to large numbers of the white American underclass. It is difficult to develop models of church growth that will reach the black masses without cultural relevancy and spirituality, which are rooted in the African American experience, while in the same vein, it is difficult to reach the white masses without cultural relevancy and evangelical fervor.

In order to reach God's people, we must speak the language of culture. In order to transform God's people we must speak the language of Christ and the Holy Spirit.

Unfortunately, cultural captivity, cultural negation, and cultural domestication of African sources and influences have resulted in the demise of numerous churches because they have failed to develop ministries that are relevant to the needs and concerns of the people living in the communities that they are called to serve. The focus, then, of the African American church in particular, and the larger mainstream church in general, must shift to *self-empowerment* and the revitalization and transformation of the people of God so as to establish a new heaven and a new earth on earth.

This model of ministry is termed *empowerment* because it emphasizes *spiritual, cultural,* and *social transformation* as bases for church growth and development. The primary purpose of the empowerment church is saving souls—having a genuine conversion experience and positively and permanently changing lives for the good of Christ and the community. The essence of empowerment, then, is the power to change and be changed spiritually; the capacity to be recipients and catalysts of positive spiritual and social transformation in all areas of black life in America. Underlying all empowerment is a spiritual growth that underscores going back to basics to win souls to Christ.

A prerequisite of empowerment and numerical growth within a church is spiritual growth and empowerment among its clergy and laity, and the conversion of the principles of ecclesia. Thus, many churches in mainline Protestantism must go back to the spiritual basics to revitalize themselves. Some churches have moved so far away from foundational spiritual principles that they have lost large numbers of members. The need, then, is not only for cultural relevance, but also for the development of basic spiritual principles that will reinvigorate the church. We must move beyond the spiritual necrophilia and spiritual thanatosis that are crippling our churches. We must go back to those foundational principles that gave mainline denominations great success in their early stages of development and will help revitalize them for the future.

Three additional presuppositions inform this model of ministry:

1. The church, as still one of the most vital and powerful institutions in black communities, *must rise up and walk* by cultivating the realization and actualization of optimum human potential for all people in every aspect of their lives. This occurs by identifying, developing, and sustaining resources and programs that will intentionally advocate *spiritual, relational,* and *communal* empowerment as a foundation for human transformation and church growth and development. For African Americans this potential is actualized on the personal and communal levels and is nurtured in the black church.

The foundation of this model of empowerment is spiritual vitality. Soul-force spirituality is at the heart of all church empowerment. If the church is to strengthen, revitalize, and grow, it must fortify its faith and spirituality.

2. As agents of transformation who are part of a perennial empowerment process, individuals are

encouraged to identify, cultivate, and translate their gifts into various ministries whose ultimate aim is the personal sanctification and positive transformation of themselves and their communities. By viewing themselves as cointentional transformers of reality, they can surmount stagnation and become more than passive observers of reality.[1] This is particularly true in United Methodism, as well as other major denominations, where a perceived system of regulatory bureaucracy and a hierarchical authority often create passivity among black and white clergy and laity that ultimately thwarts their capacity to become positive change agents both within their churches and within surrounding communities.

3. Empowerment ministries utilize human, material, and spiritual resources within and outside of the church to establish a cooperative network of civic, business, and spiritual leaders in the community. The ultimate objective is to forge an alliance between these groups that establishes a community-based consortium that moves the church beyond its four walls, and to demonstrate concern for the community by addressing its critical needs.

The resulting reciprocity between church and community helps establish the church as a spiritual life and community center, and develops a collaborative covenant empowering both the church and community. As the quintessential empowerment center of the community, the black church is responsible for identifying, developing, and enhancing those critical resources necessary to the survival of both church and community.

The purpose, then, is to cultivate models of ministry that stress positive, cooperative action between the church and community. Too often some black mainstream churches have ignored the needs of their surrounding communities out of fear and ignorance, and have fostered codependency and passivity among parishioners through *theologies of maintenance* rather than *theologies of empowerment.*

Moreover, an additional problem is the pathological obsession with tending to church structures and politics that distract mainstream churches from their mission of transformation. Whereas maintaining churches is not particularly problematic in itself, churches within United Methodism and other mainstream Protestant denominations must begin reenvisioning and reconfiguring themselves by developing more relevant and viable ministries that speak to the whole person by addressing their emotional, spiritual, social, environmental, vocational, educational, political, economic, cultural, familial, and institutional needs. The gospel calls us to grow. We grow by offering people something of value and by cultivating spiritual and practical resources that will enable them to become change agents in their homes, families, and communities. By developing this new approach, we can pilot programs that will revitalize not only individual churches, but the denominations we serve as well.

Empowerment ministries quite simply call the people of God back to spiritual and ecclesiastical basics by developing ministries that optimize human potential through training, nurturing, healing, and education for human wholeness. It is ministry for the poor, oppressed, misused, abused, the haves and have nots, the influential and affluent, as well as the talented and gifted of American society. It is ministry that addresses the whole person and essentially reestablishes the church as a pivotal force for change and renewal in the world. It is ministry that captures the best of the evangelical and intellectual traditions of the Christian church for the transformation and empowerment of the larger culture and society.

As mainline institutional churches hurdle past the

century mark, they must become more creative, resourceful, and dynamic if they are to address the demands and needs of the new millennium. Churches can ill afford to have for-members-only, country-club approaches to ministry or simply cultivate narcissistic, navel-gazing theologies that are always inward looking and never outward reaching.

Empowerment ministries invariably reach out for the common good. The time has come for new ecclesiastical models that will place mainline churches on the cutting edge of positive change not only by simply shaping ministry around future trends, but by proactively rather than reactively developing models of ministry that will speak to the whole needs of persons. As we move further into the frontier of a new millennium, the church must possess the courage to become the harbinger of change, renewal, and hope for the people of God.

Although written from an African American viewpoint, *The Empowerment Church* is applicable to pastors and laypeople of every race, context, or culture. Anyone interested in helping the church address the needs of people and their communities will find the information included here of use.

CHAPTER ONE

Jesus' Ministry of Empowerment

Jesus' ministry was certainly one of empowerment. A central axiom of Jesus' ministry was that he unequivocally and positively changed lives for the better by calling people who were conflicted and afflicted into a profound realization of their spiritual resources. In addition, Jesus made them aware of their God-centered potential, which not only forever changed their lives, but also the communities in which they lived.

Inherent in his ministry was a process of *empowerment* actualized through personal intervention and spiritual transformation. Whether touching, healing, rebuking, exhorting, preaching, teaching, or reaching, Jesus' ministry had great impact on the people of his time. This ministry of outreach and love, which invariably awakened within the individual awareness of God's transformative and redemptive grace, compelled the afflicted into a deeper awareness of the true power of God in their lives. No longer were they simply the passive recipients of God's miraculous intercession, but instead they brought others to Christ through the credence and efficacy of their apostolic witness and the power of the Holy Spirit. They too, after touching and being with Jesus, could envision themselves as agents of transformation and spiritual grace and power. Any previous notions of human failings and frailities that stifled potential were eclipsed after an encounter with Christ.

Moreover, Jesus' ministry heralded the redemptive possibilities of human community. His ministry of transformation and empowerment was actualized ultimately for the restoration of the human community, bringing oneness with God and wholeness with others. The sense of wholeness and fulfillment Jesus conferred upon the afflicted was designed to bring them back into the community from which they had been estranged. This wholeness and oneness that they experienced grew out of a longing for spiritual growth and empowerment.

Spiritual empowerment thus enabled the individual to exceed his or her greatest self-expectations. Whereas community empowerment gauged how well the individual was able to reestablish himself or herself within the larger society and how well the spiritual principles that had been learned were translated into community transformation, individual healing and redemption ultimately led to the transformation and empowerment of the social collective as a unifying and totalizing force for positive change. In Jesus' ministry, individual empowerment always had larger communal ramifications.

At the heart of all empowerment is *spiritual growth* and *faith*. Accordingly, present-day church empowerment models must equally benefit the communities they serve. Not only is it important for *individuals* to be transformed, healed, redeemed, and restored, but they must also translate the power actualized individually through their encounter with Christ into the collective meliorations of community. No longer is it enough to simply run and shout and be healed and have the Holy Ghost on Sunday morning. The ultimate question becomes: How do we translate that power of awareness, vitality, and transcendence into the radical transformation of community? Empowerment processes facilitate such transformation.

The central objectives of Jesus' ministry were to:

- positively transform people's lives
- connect them with their most important spiritual resources
- increase their knowledge, faith, and awareness of God's possibilities through their own actualized potential
- empower them to translate that awareness into meaningful action within the larger human community

He achieved this through basic spiritual teaching, training, and witness by emphasizing fundamentals or basic foundational principles. The extent to which the afflicted within the community realized their potential was the point at which the larger community actualized its own potential as a collective entity. This gave the early followers of the way enormous momentum and power. Their ability to interpret and translate that redemptive, transformative awareness through Christ into human community has made Christianity a vital force for spiritual and social change for the past twenty centuries.

Jesus' ministry changed people, things, and conditions. It transformed the social and religious order, the moral trajectory of the universe, and ultimately, the course of human history. No life could remain dormant or indifferent after an encounter with Christ. Moreover, the lives he changed also changed others, for a central tenet of being a follower of the way is not only to be touched by Christ, to experience deep and enduring change within, but also to touch others in his name.

What were the prominent empowerment characteristics of Jesus' ministry that can serve as a foundation for empowerment ministry in the present context?

1. Jesus taught people foundational principles of spirituality that enabled them to see their own spiritual tra-

ditions in new ways and to conceptualize new possibilities of God in new spiritual frameworks.

2. Jesus' ministry transformed people's spiritual perception and understanding of God through personal revelation, intervention, and interaction with people. Encountering Jesus meant that persons were compelled to alter their ideas of God. God was no longer inactively remote from the daily struggles of people. God now walked, talked, and lived with them each day in a more personal way.

3. Jesus transformed the concept of people in relationship with God. They no longer viewed themselves as passive objects of God's will or as people wholly incapable of positively influencing their social environment and milieu. They now saw themselves as cointentional catalysts for positive change. By seeing themselves differently, they saw society differently or began acting to transform that society into an ideal faith community.

4. Jesus directly, as well as vicariously, transformed communities by providing individuals with the spiritual elements of positive change and renewal. Not only did the recipients of Jesus' power and grace experience change within, but their communities were also changed by the power of their testimonies of Christ's work in their lives.

Thus, through the sheer magnitude of his spiritual power, presence, and intercession, Jesus forever altered people's understanding of their own abilities and God's possibilities. He modified the structures of spiritual consciousness through the power of his revelation by actualizing the self and its potential through sacrificial and redeeming love. By transforming people's understanding of God, Jesus changed their focus from their disabilities to their true gifts and capacities, enabling them to recenter themselves spiritually, recreate themselves cognitively, and reclaim that vital God-center as the central fount of their identity and being. The result was an elevation of people's self-esteem through God's redemptive possibilities and an increase in those who became active witnesses and agents of transformation in their communities. Although Jesus admonished them against telling others, the fact that numerous individuals went into the larger community and shared what Jesus had said, demonstrated their desire to share the power and joy of personal transformation with the larger community.

During Jesus' lifetime, people were often defined by their disabilities. Moreover, people with physical infirmities and afflictions were labeled *sinners*. In many cases, these designations were so psychologically and spiritually debilitating that individuals were seldom able to surmount the stigmas forced upon them. Jesus' ministry of empowerment gave people a new understanding of themselves and of what God could do through them by encouraging them to view their disabilities as *descriptions* of their human condition rather than as *definitions* of their personhood and capacities to face and solve their problems. Although the larger society defined and measured their humanity, human potential, and self-worth by their physical disabilities, Jesus dismissed and dispelled such crippling notions as erroneous and untenable.

By emphasizing the love of God, Jesus reconfigured the understanding of God's power and potential in transforming the afflicted's condition. People were no longer defined by the larger society or religious establishment, but saw themselves as persons of ultimate worth, spiritual power, and social purpose. Armed with this new understanding of themselves and God, they could psychologically, spiritually, and socially surmount the barriers to full personhood. Basically, Jesus transfigured people's consciousness of God, themselves, and their capacity as empowered and transformed persons to change their communities. By changing self-awareness through increased consciousness of potential, people could alter those external social conditions that fostered and perpetuated their psychological and physical debilitation.

The essence of empowerment is to help people understand that with Christ they can become the catalysts for their own spiritual and social transformation. To think and do for self and others without being hindered by the debilitating constraints that bind, defeat, and ultimately destroy people's capacity to transform themselves and others is a principal objective of the empowerment process.

A great hallmark of Jesus' power ministry is that it set the stage for a permanent revolution that continues today. This revolution shifted the axis of power from religious and political institutions to the individual by providing each person with an experience of God that radically altered his or her sense of self and her or his possibilities. The imperative, then, is to translate that awareness into concrete action that will ultimately benefit the individual and community of which he or she is integrally related and intimately connected.

In light of this, it is important that churches today establish the same empowerment foundations for ministry. It is axiomatic that Jesus' ministry made something happen spiritually at both the core and periphery of individual lives and their communities. Present-day churches and denominations must also make something happen spiritually and practically in the lives of God's people and in the communities they serve. Through the movement and empowerment of the Holy Spirit and by going back to spiritual basics and the foundations of faith, they can also make something happen. Rather than simply wait, maintain, or ignore the problems and concerns of their communities, congregations must actively engage in ministries of revitalization and uplift for the people of God.

The mainline church can ill afford to further cultivate an ethos where pastors passively wait for permission from church officials to tell them how to empower their churches and communities. To be Christian is to be empowered and to empower others. Emulating the empowerment model of Jesus, churches can avoid the malaise and atrophy that threatens to dissipate ministries throughout mainline Protestant denominations.

CHAPTER TWO

Toward a Model of
Spiritual Empowerment

In *The Purpose Driven Church,* Rick Warren says that in order for a church to grow it must become healthy.[1] Moreover, attaining a wholesome, winsome spirituality is indispensable to becoming healthy. Equally important is that numerical growth in congregations must be preceded by spiritual growth among its clergy and laity. Too often we speak of numerical growth without addressing the fundamental spiritual needs of people. Not every church will experience a quantum growth in membership. Every church will not grow into megamembership. However, the large number of unchurched people in America is an indicator that every church has the potential to increase its membership by several thousands. Although quantum numerical growth may not be achievable, every church can experience some measure of spiritual growth, which is the foundation for healthy congregations.

"Come Holy Ghost!"
Reclaiming a Tradition of Holiness

In many mainline liberal Protestant denominations there appears to be a culture of disdain or contempt for using the language of spirituality and a culture of holiness as a basis for spiritual interaction and empowerment. Moreover, there seems to be an absence of a genuine invocation of the presence and power of the Holy Ghost in church affairs. I was shocked to discover at the beginning of my pastorate at Hope United Methodist Church how secular the church had become and how the language of spirituality was wholly absent from the vocabulary of parishioners. This was also true of our regional church meetings and gatherings. Any mention of the Holy Spirit to guide the judgment, direction, and renewal of the church was sternly rebuked.

How could the mention of the Holy Spirit or Holy Ghost within the church cause such shame and discomfort on the part of some parishioners? How could members and clergy be seduced into believing that the language of spirituality has no real place in the church, and that to use such words illicits scorn, resentment, and amusement from certain people in the church? Why does public prayer and even the mention or invocation of the name and presence of Jesus in the life and conduct of the church make some people so uncomfortable? Has the church become so secular that any use of spiritual language is now an abomination? Such discomfort in using the language of holiness seems particularly manifest in mainline middle-class Protestant denominations. Even some predominantly black denominations appear to be relatively uncomfortable in ostensibly and unapologetically referencing the Holy Ghost as a source of strength, joy, and power in church life.

Edmund Robb makes this startling observation about mainline churches in general:

> The Liberal Church has responded to the secular challenge with accommodation rather than confrontation. The mainline churches have retreated each time they have been challenged until it is difficult to tell the difference between the secular humanist and the liberal Christian. It seems that we are more influenced by secu-

lar ideology than Christian theology. We will not grow by seeking approval from an enlightened secular society by coming to the world and saying, "We are not so different from you." We will grow and influence the world when we challenge its claims and boldly insist on the uniqueness of Christianity and the non-negotiable truths of the faith.[2]

Early in my pastorate I recall being slightly reprimanded by a parishioner who was annoyed because I began my prayers with "Come, Holy Ghost," and ended them with "In the name of Jesus." Any open mention of Jesus for this individual was problematic. If we are truly Christians who are seeking the light, the presence, and the power of the Holy Spirit, why should we be ashamed of Christ and the gospel? Should not the presence of the Holy Spirit lead and guide us not only in the church but in every area of our lives? Since when did publicly referencing the Holy Spirit go out of style or become a source of consternation? Should not spirituality and holiness be principal elements of our spiritual and theological vocabulary and culture? Should we not unabashedly call upon the name of Jesus, invoke the Holy Ghost's presence, power, and guidance into church life as we seek to tell others and build God's kingdom?

The church looks too much like the world in the way it thinks and does the business of God's ministry. It appears to have lost its spiritual power. A kind of pagan choke hold seems to be fastened upon the neck of the church where all things spiritual appear to be wholly out of place and the Holy Ghost appears to be unwelcome.

Needed today is a church that is unafraid to invoke the presence of the Holy Ghost, reference the name of Jesus ostensibly and unapologetically in open air, and cultivate a climate of holiness. Until we can comfortably use the language of spirituality, we cannot comfortably attain the consciousness of Christian spirituality because language reflects consciousness and consciousness reflects being. I am not advocating that every other word ought to be "Thank you, Jesus" or "Praise the Lord," but there should be a measure of assurance and comfort with the Holy Spirit's presence and power, and in using the language of spirituality as a reference for who we are as people of God. Invoking and beckoning the Holy Spirit's presence in church life should not cause discomfort, dismay, or embarrassment for the true believer. Why should we feel ashamed of inviting the Holy Ghost to have presence in our lives?

One pastor recalled his experience with parishioners engaging in spiritual semantics about whether *Holy Spirit* or *Holy Ghost* were apropos terms of usage. One remarked that *ghost* suggested something scary or spooky and that the word *spirit* was more viable. The other stated that the word *ghost* was much more descriptive of the ephemeral nature of the Holy Spirit and seemed to be much more inclusive of the all-encompassing nature of God. *Spirit,* in this person's estimation, was less intimidating than the word *ghost. Spirit* was a part of the Holy Ghost's attributes.

Neither were ashamed of making reference to the Holy Ghost or Holy Spirit as part of their spiritual vocabulary. The fact that they debated the issue signified both their passion and concern for being more spiritual and called attention to the importance of the language of spirituality as a part of their daily Christian discourse.

Conversely, there are those who are simply uncomfortable using either term. Some forms of piety exhort quietistic reservation, reticence, and awe in relation to the Holy Spirit. Because of God's profundity, sanctity, and majesty, one dares not speak of the Holy Spirit too glibly or loosely. Much like the Hebrew high priests who were forbidden from speaking the name *Yahweh* in the Sanctum Sanctorum, many Christians have been taught to make only sparing reference to the Holy Ghost. You can tell a lot about people by the language they use and the things they reference in their conversation. It is unfortunate that many Christians, black and white, have been lured into being defensive about referencing God or the Holy Spirit in their dialogue with others.

Still others in mainstream liberal Protestant denominations have become so erudite, educated, and intellectual that speaking of the Holy Ghost or Holy Spirit is just too mundane, frivolous, callow, fundamental, evangelical, and downright simple. This aversion, as Richard Hoftstadter and Mark Noll affirm, may be a response to the anti-intellectualism of the modern Protestant evangelical spirit.[3] Perhaps we shun the evangelical label and the specter of its various associations because as trained clergy and laity we pride ourselves on being students of the Enlightenment.

Intellectualism and scholarship have very important roles in our understanding of who we are as Christians. John Wesley emphasized reason and the mind as important parts of the Methodist quadrilateral.[4] The mind and reason can be used to glorify God, but we can also maintain a simple spirituality that gives us passion, power, and reason. Mark Noll also says that many of the great evangelical thinkers had great minds and used their intellects to glorify God. The problem is with the anti-intellectualism of the American evangelical enterprise.[5]

For numerous mainliners, spiritual language consists of God-laden words that make people feel silly.[6] "It is for the simpleminded who take their religion too simply," quipped one man. "We are beyond such things!" said another. "We just can't bring ourselves to say such ridiculous things. We are not Holy Rollers! We are not Bible-toters! We are not finger-pointers!"[7]

But in our striving to be holy should we not use the language of holiness? Would not John Wesley, himself, urge us to be holy, to speak and live the language of Christian holiness? We must, however, not confuse *holiness* with *holier than thou-ness* or the *I am better than you-ness* that often characterizes the quest to be holy and spiritual. Could it be that our middle-class predilections and higher education have prompted us to disdain and negate the fundamental language of our faith so that many of us feel discomfort or shame in invoking the Holy Ghost's presence and power in our lives?

What is wrong with holiness? What is wrong with being on fire for the Lord? Has holiness gone out of style, taken a backseat to the secular humanism and paganism of our modern culture and society? Can we not rebuild and revise our spiritual lexicon in order to reemphasize the importance of spiritual empowerment? What has happened to our spirituality? Why does it look so much like the world we live in, which is largely unholy?

In order for the church to grow numerically it must grow spiritually. In order to grow spiritually it must grow beyond the constraints and barriers that prevent it from realizing and practicing the presence of Christ. Thus the church must adopt a language of spirituality that invokes the power and presence of the Holy Ghost in daily experience and uses this Spirit as the ultimate reference point for behavior, guidance, and belief.

Come, Holy Spirit! Come, Holy Ghost! Fall fresh upon us! Teach us to not be ashamed of thy presence. Give us a mind and heart to serve thee and to live according to thy ways. If the church is to be empowered, it must reclaim the centrality of the Holy Spirit's presence in its mission and ministry. This means a willingness to reference and index the Holy Ghost as comforter and catalyst for kingdom building and to reinsert the language of holiness into the lexicon of the church. We must break out of the current captivity of cultural and secular constraint that binds us to the sensibilities of the world and holds us hostage to practices and beliefs that repress our expressive spirituality.

Naming Our Sin and Evil and Not Shaking Hands with the Devil

Another important step in becoming a spiritually empowered church is recognizing individual and corporate sin and calling evil *evil*. Have we lost our spirit of discernment by which we are able to differentiate what is good and what is evil? In my experience in numerous churches there is almost a pathological aversion or avoidance to calling evil what it is. We need to learn to name our sin and the sins of others and then address it. Some people are just evil. Some things are just evil. Some people are on a mission to destroy and undermine the church. They have entrenched themselves in leadership or other places of authority in the church and for years have wielded authority to the church's detriment and demise. In our desire as clergy and laity to serve, love, forgive, and redeem, we often gloss over the evil deeds of ourselves and others. Although we can often refrain from making judgment about the evildoing of ourselves and others, the truth is this unwillingness to call evil out is only to the devil's advantage. The devil can hide out in the church, take up residency in the church, and eventually destroy or close a church because of our unwillingness to address evil. The devil relies on our reticence, our failure to expose him for what he is. Our failure to call him out and name his deeds protects his interests.

If you look within the walls of numerous churches to determine the reasons for stagnation and lack of growth, somewhere you find evil persons and evil intentions. The problem is that good, God-loving, church-serving people often avoid confrontation with evil. Rather than stand up to evil and challenge it through love, we give in to it and cooperate with it often to the demise of the church. It is better to stand up to evil than to compromise and go to bed with it. Acquiescing to evil does the church more harm than good for the long haul.

One pastor related the problem of wresting the church's financial records from the former treasurer, who would neither submit to an audit nor turn over the books to the newly appointed treasurer.[8] The pastor became concerned when checks written to creditors began to bounce. Eventually, the pastor and church took the former treasurer to court. When the books were finally retrieved, it was discovered that the woman had written personal checks using the church's account. Moreover, she had taken several expensive cruises and had squandered some of the church's most precious resources and reserves. This woman did an evil thing, and her failure to acknowledge and repent of her sin precipitated her ouster as treasurer and her eventual prosecution.

It is important that in developing a theology that names our sin and the sin of others that we discern between the evil deed and the evil person. It is true that some people are just evil. For many of us, as sinners, we are capable of doing something evil or wrong in God's eyes. Although we are all capable of performing evil acts, we may not necessarily be evil persons. However, we should confront evil with firmness and compassion, remembering that persons are still worthy of God's redemptive love and grace. We must always hold out the possibility of forgiveness and redemption for those who commit evil, especially when they manifest a spirit of confession and repentance. We must also never fail to put ourselves on trial for the evil and sin we do.

My concern is more for people who make a life's vocation or career out of raising hell and wreaking havoc in God's church. Their practice of evil is so crafty, demonic, and deceitful that it appears to be innocent of all wrong-doing. This type of evil is seldom flagrant or blatant, but sly and chicanerous. These are people who smile in your face and stab you in your back. They fake left and go right. They are foxy and cunning and will use every device to prevent the ministry from going forward. Often they say they support a program, then work to kill it. They pretend that they are good workers, yet everything they do undermines the church's ministry and creates discord and discontent among parishioners.

The problem is there is good in evil people and there is evil in good people. Evil people are seldom all wrong. *Nothing is all wrong. Even a clock that has stopped is right twice a day.* The problem is they have just enough good to make you think they are not evil. The problem with good people is that they have just enough evil to make you wonder if they are good.

Failure to develop a theology that recognizes the reality of sin, evil, and the demonic disarms and prevents the church from eradicating its sins and ills. In order for the church to be spiritually empowered it cannot afford to look the other way when the devil shows up. We must be careful not to omit the reality of the demonic and evil because it can devastate the church. In other words, don't shake hands with the devil and try to befriend him. Don't be tricked into thinking that the devil and his demons no longer exist. God is not pleased, and the people of God will pay dearly for it. The devil counts on our failure to name our sin and to call him out for his evil work in the church.

Converting the Church to Christ

The Wesleyan scholar Albert Outler makes the following poignant observation:

What happens to men [and women] who hear the gospel, who confess Jesus Christ as Lord, who join the church and then sink into a spiritual slump under the numbing weight of nominal, formal, perfunctory Christianity? We know very well what happens and it convicts us all of a monumental hypocrisy. In more instances than we can bring ourselves to admit, the local congregation is simply not a healthy setting for a new-born Christian to be initiated into with any lively hope of growing up in Christ, "in holiness and righteous-ness," etc. Having come to bear the name of Christ as his badge of identity, he often comes to wear it in name only—which is, of course, what "nominal Christianity" means.[9]

Obstacles to church empowerment and spiritual growth range from the seven last words, *we never did it that way before,* to the inability to adapt to change. At a church growth conference, I was asked what the church needed to grow. My response was, "a conversion experi-ence." The church, believe it or not, needs to be converted to Christ. We presuppose that the church is practicing the teachings, presence, and mind of Christ, but this is not always the case. In many instances, what is often practiced are the organized forms of institutional ecclesi-ology, which sponsor the praxis of original religion. We thus practice religion that is organized and regulated by church institutions. Being religious does not mean we are spiritual. Belonging to the church and practicing ecclesiology does not mean we are living the teachings of Jesus. Being organized religiously and practicing regula-tory ecclesiology does not mean we have been converted to Christ. Going to church does not mean that we are saved; that we are living in a saving relationship with Christ. Many people in the church have an opinion of God, but not a saving relationship with God. Many peo-ple in the church are practicing secularized versions of organized religion under the auspices of a particular denomination, but they are not practicing Christ. The church needs to be converted to Christ. The people need a saving relationship with Jesus!

Often people are converted to a denomination, a church, or a specific style of preaching, worship, and fellowship. They are wooed by the culture of a particular church rather than transformed for and by Christ. Because their friends and neighbors attend church, they attend church. They attend church because it feels good, looks good socially, or holds out the promises or prospects of feeling good in some ecstatic, relational, or communal way.

What they have not experienced is a conversion to Christ or what Outler refers to as "a growing up in Christ." Wesley himself spoke of his Aldersgate experience where his heart was strangely warmed. What some have not experienced is movement from the practice of Christianity as a part-time avocation or hobby to a full-time vocation, so they need a complete, thoroughgoing conversion experience. They need their hearts "strangely warmed."[10] They need to be positively changed from the inside out. They need to be saved. They need an "inside job." They need a *reconversion experience.* Interior sanctification should invariably lead to exterior transformation.

Churches need to be reconverted from old habits that die hard and behaviors that thwart the Holy Spirit's presence and power to convert, save, and change lives. Clergy and laity need to be converted from the myopic, provincial, and parochial forms of consciousness that constrict ministry and truly stymie growth in the Word and Spirit. Movement from the seven last words, *we never did it that way before,* to the seventeen most important words, *there is no limit to what you can do if you don't mind who gets the credit,* can help a church move beyond the spiritual and practical limitations that stagnate growth.

How can the church truly be empowered or empower others when it has not experienced at its core and periphery a genuine conversion to Christ? How can the church be truly empowered when it is more secular than sacred, more social than spiritual, more pagan than pious? How can the church become a spiritual empowerment center when it is ambivalent about the use of spiritual language and shuns the more fundamental foundational evangelistic styles of ministry? How can the church effectively convert others to Christ if it seldom invokes the Holy Ghost, gives cursory emphasis to gifts and graces, never accentuates tithing and stewardship as part of Christian responsibility, and is so busy tending to the bureaucracy of maintaining church structures that it cannot invite unsaved souls unto Christ to be saved?

What Happened to Saving Souls?

In order for the church to call the unsaved unto Christ it must be saved and reconverted to Christ. The church must experience at its core a fundamental conversion of values and beliefs that will empower it unto salvation. Regrettably, I can count on one hand the occasions I have heard references made in larger denominational circles or even in local churches to saving souls. We just don't talk about these things anymore. Have they gone out of style? They are antiquated, archaic, fundamental forms of religiosity that are too simplistic, anti-intellectual, and nonsecular for our modern sensibilities and beliefs.

Survey the worship services of many mainline churches and you will find that few have a hymn of invitation that invites people to Christ for salvation after the proclamation. Even more disconcerting is that people join churches like they clandestinely join clubs and social organizations! They no longer join the church during the worship service, after the Word is preached and while they are under the anointing of the Holy Ghost! They join in other ways, in secret, out of the worship purview of the faith community and the watchful eye of parishioners who can begin the membership nurturing process.

While a student intern working in a local United Methodist church in Chicago, the district superintendent and supervising pastor administered a survey asking church leaders and members to prioritize the church's fundamental mission. Out of the one hundred people surveyed, not one mentioned saving souls as a priority of the church. Everything from selecting leaders to paying apportionments to maintaining church structures was cited, but not salvation and certainly not saving souls.

The church needs a conversion to Christ. Are we serving churches where salvation is no longer relevant, where the language of spirituality is so repulsive that we seldom make reference to Christ in fear of peer rebuke? If the church is not calling the unsaved unto Christ to be saved, what, then, *is* the church? What distinguishes the church from a country, social, or auxiliary club? Why does the church look more like the world than the world? Why do some churches not even invite people to Christ during Sunday morning worship?

The church cannot afford to be a spiritual halfway house for the unconverted and unsaved. It can least afford to be led by almost-Christians who are half-baked at best in their enthusiasm for Christ. In affirming that the church should be converted to Christ, what actually do we mean?

1. Not only should individuals repent of their sin, but the church as a corporate entity should also repent of its sin, accept Jesus Christ, and be saved.

2. The church should preach and teach the power of salvation and the power of Christ to save souls.
3. The church should invite the presence of the Holy Ghost to guide and direct all its affairs.
4. The teachings, ministry, and life of Christ should become the ultimate reference, ground, or guide for the church's mission and ministry in the community and the world.
5. The church should implement viable programs of Christian training where clergy, leaders, and laity are taught the fundamental precepts of Christian character, service, and conduct. Bible study, prayer, and other spiritual disciplines should be taught as a means of empowering the congregation in the witness of the Word.
6. The church should commit to discipling others to Christ.
7. The church should become a center of love, redemption, and hospitality where the lost, rejected, and despised are given safe harbor. The gospel of salvation must be translated into good works on behalf of the larger community.

Our fundamental task, as the church, is to create a culture, ethos, or environment where the people of God can grow spiritually in the Word, in service and witness to the congregation and community, and in every area of their lives. Salvation means empowerment. To convert the church to Christ is to empower the church to actualize the true potential that Christ has given it. This means that the presence, power, and practice of the Holy Spirit are welcomed. It means people are encouraged to cultivate spiritual gifts so as to bear spiritual fruit. It means cultivating a climate where the Word of God can take root in the hearts, minds, and souls of the people of God, and the Holy Spirit can direct them in the enterprise of ministry.

To convert the church essentially means to transform it from an institutional organization preoccupied with survival to a living organism whose vitality is empowered by the Word of God, a living Christ, and the Holy Ghost. Because the church is so preoccupied with structure, it has lost some of the spiritual power and focus. Richard Wilke in *And Are We Yet Alive?* says:

> Perhaps it is our nearsightedness that has made us a church turned inward. Our energies and resources are expended internally. The machinery of the church receives unbelievable attention; we scurry about oiling the wheels of the organizational structure. . . . But now our methodology approaches madness, our organizational genius consumes our most sophisticated talent. Our structure has become an end in itself, not a means of saving the world.[11]

John Wesley in 1786 warned against Methodists becoming a dead sect, having the form of religion without the power.[12] Other denominations would do well to also heed this warning.

We know that sin estranges us from God. Here we are cut off from the main power source because we lack obedience to Christ. "Not mine will, but thine will be done" should be part of the mission statement of every church. Moreover, the church should ask: Is saving souls our primary mission? Are we modeling salvation in our behavior, belief, mission, and ministry? Are we practicing Christian precepts and principles in our daily experience and our relations with one another? Are we modeling Christian character in the congregation and larger community?

The problem is that every institution claiming to be a church is not practicing the teachings of Jesus or inviting the presence of the Holy Spirit into its daily affairs. In contrast, every church truly of Christ should manifest

some form of spiritual empowerment as a basis for winning souls to Christ. People should experience some
form of renewal, power, or redemption in some aspect of
their lives. It is true that we have all sinned and fallen
short of the glory of God, but the danger is in churches
"passing" for a genuine faith community—a church in
name only. Such "churches" are not building up the
Body of Christ and the kingdom of God, but tearing
down and destroying lives. Congregations are playing
church and negating God.

A church converted to Christ exalts Christ and saving
souls as the center and source of its power and authority.
A church that is converted to Christ is not ashamed of
the gospel. It preaches, teaches, and outreaches the Word
of God. It not only worships Christ during Sunday services, but follows Christ during the week. It often real-
izes that the most important part of Christian service is
not what occurs in Sunday worship but what happens
between the benediction of the previous week's service
and the invocation of the next week's service.

What flourishes in numerous churches is not the
reality of Christ whose life and teachings constitute the
foundation of the church's mission and ministry, but a
cult of the preacher or laity, a cult of tradition, or a particular power group whose sole purpose is to rule others
and control the church for personal purposes. Such
churches take the name of God in vain because they are
no more converted to Christ or committed to practicing
Christ than the avowed hypocrite or atheist. Strong
words indeed, but this is the truth of the matter.

These churches are in great need of a conversion and
reconversion experience. A conversion to the principles,
praxis, and teachings of Christ is necessary since much
of Christianity has lapsed into a diligent practice of
organized religion rather than true Christian spirituality.
A conversion to the idea that saving souls remains one of

the most important priorities of the church is needed. A conversion to Christ, however, presupposes a desire to have more than just an opinion of Christ, but a living dialogical relationship with him. The church must therefore retrieve those elements of spirituality that will empower it to transform lives in the name of Jesus Christ. Conversion and reconversion are important aspects of revitalizing churches spiritually.

The Church Should Corporately Repent of Its Sins

We exhort poor sinners to repent of their sins, but what about the corporate church? If the church is to be spiritually empowered it must also confess, repent, redeem, forgive others, and be forgiven. Such repentance should not only occur in local congregations but also within denominations. The sins of individuals are one thing. The sins of institutions are quite another. Recently, The United Methodist Church held a service of healing and repentance for the sin of racism, which offered denominational officials and laity an opportunity to confess the sin of racism, apologize, and receive forgiveness for it. It also sent the signal that the church was willing to take a long hard look at itself and be redeemed by starting anew.

Each local congregation should repent of its sins of omission and commission. It could be the sin of not allowing new people of different races and cultures to comfortably attend and belong to the church, the sin of not following up on members who have been sick and shut in and who have left the church, the sin of not feeding the hungry and helping the poor, or the sin of not reaching out to the larger community and creating an open-door policy that addresses the ultimate concerns of the community. It could be the sin of hard-heartedness and nonforgiveness, or the failure to recognize women as worthy servants of God.

Some churches have allowed a culture of contempt and recrimination to flourish rather than a climate of healing, forgiveness, and redemption. People need to confess and repent and be healed. The church also needs to confess, repent, and receive a healing touch from Jesus Christ. Some churches cannot revitalize themselves because they have not said, "We are sorry," or "Please forgive us for our sins of omission and commission," or what the Catholics call our mortal and venal sins.

If some white churches should repent for the sin of racism, then many black churches should repent for the sin of sexism through the subordination of women in church, and intraclassism culminating in various forms of discrimination among black people in church. It is true that many black churches are largely comprised of females, who hold leadership roles in the church, but the attitude toward clergy-women by some male clergy is both an anathema and an insult to the God who has called and anointed women for ministry.

Who are we to stand in God's way and say who or who is not worthy to be called a servant of God? This is playing God. Too many black male preachers along with their parishioners, both female and male, have created a climate of hostility and contempt for female clergy, and the black church should repent of this sin. The church needs to be healed and redeemed from this practice. How can the church grow spiritually as God would have it when clergy and laity are playing God? Additionally, some black churches should repent for the sin of classism and intragroup discrimination based upon skin color. For years it was highly believed that the lighter one's skin color the more favored one was in the eyes of white society. Unfortunately, some churches still play the skin game where only the "lightie bright" are welcomed and the "blackie dark" are not.

Calling the church to repentance does not mean blame-gaming other churches, races, cultures, and peoples for their sins, but is a time for examining, confessing, and repenting of our own sins and failures. Both the black and the white churches should repent for the way they have canonized, regulated, bureaucratized, and enshrined their sins into shameful institutional practices. Both churches should repent for their various abuses of ecclesiastical power.

If genuine spiritual growth, power, and prosperity is to emerge in all churches, there must be a healthy respect for all persons who have been gifted by God to serve in ministry. The local and corporate church should repent of its sins.

Spiritual empowerment is essential for the revitalization of the church, and the church should corporately and collectively ask God's forgiveness for its sins. This is a positive step toward restoring the spiritual health and vitality of local congregations and larger denominations.

Returning to the Wesleyan Revival Spirit and Word-Centeredness in Church Life

B.Y.O.B. and Banishing Scriptural Illiteracy

Equally important in developing a model of spiritual empowerment for local churches is a retrieval of the best of the Wesleyan evangelical revival traditions. We need not reinvent the wheel, but simply go back and discover vital dimensions of our evangelical roots as a faith community. James C. Logan says:

> To appropriate the Wesleyan tradition in our time does not call for a repristinated Wesleyansim. Such an effort of

reappropriation requires a critical dialogue with that very tradition. Rather than repeating Wesley's own words and structures of thought, which really belong to the eighteenth century, we must seek to discover trajectories from that tradition which can inform, inspire, and direct us as faithful participants in the tradition in a new day.[13]

This includes evangelism and practical spirituality that affirms the study and practice of God's Word as essential to Christian growth and character. Wesley viewed the Bible as a quintessential resource and ultimate authority in the cultivation of Christian spirituality, faith, and belief. His ministry contained six fundamental traits that empowered growth in word and witness among the Methodist society: Bible literacy, conversion experience, evangelical outreach, cultural fluency, spiritual discipline, and prophetic consciousness. "Toward the end of his career (1786), Wesley reemphasized this . . . that the Bible is the whole and sole rule of Christian faith and practice. . . . For this reason Wesley would not allow any other authority to stand either above or on par with Scripture."[14]

The centrality of Word-centeredness and diligent study of scriptures was an important part of Wesleyan theology. *Scripture* as the ultimate authority played a vital role in calling the people back to God and raising the consciousness of faith in the Christian community. Wesley also understood that the church must *outreach* into the community and that the success of this outreach would largely depend upon the efficacy in which the gospel was presented, as well as the way it was packaged in the idioms of culture that the people could grasp. Cultural fluency is important because we must present the gospel within the familiarity of a particular culture if the people are to understand it. George Hunter calls this an "indigenous approach" to ministry.[15]

Spiritual disciplines, such as prayer and Bible study, were essential components of spiritual formation. *Prophetic consciousness,* which emphasized the transformation of individuals and societies more than calling political powers into account for their negligence of the poor, and spiritual conversion or being born again were hallmarks of the Wesleyan movement.

Unbeknownst to Wesley, many of the religious and spiritual reforms instituted by the religious praxis of the new Wesleyan movement eventually led to major social transformations in English and American society. Moreover, Wesley's antislavery views were influential upon people such as William Wilberforce, and the abolitionist movement in Great Britain had vestiges of influence on the American antislavery movement.

The point here is that scriptural illiteracy is a bane that is undermining the spiritual authority and power of local congregations. Wesley stressed the importance of scripture, but regrettably many churches have failed to train their members in basic Bible precepts. An incident early in my pastorate provided a clue about the magnitude of this problem. While teaching Bible study, I asked a church leader to turn to 1 Corinthians. Instead, she turned to 1 Chronicles.

Many so-called Christians do not value their Bibles, seldom read them, and often have never purchased them. My philosophy is *B.Y.O.B. Buy your own Bible. Browse your own Bible. Believe in the Bible. Bring your Bible to church.* The number of churches where Bible study is not taught or venerated as an integral part of spiritual formation is shocking.

Scriptural illiteracy is hampering our churches. The failure to teach and preach Bible study as part of daily devotion and spiritual formation has, in many instances, zapped the Spirit and killed numerous churches. I have lost count of the conversations I have had with *good*

United Methodists and those of other denominations who have expressed discomfort in bringing their Bibles to church or reading their Bibles daily. Instead, they come to Sunday worship and pull the Bible from the pew when the sermon texts are read, but refuse to purchase their own Bible or read it for daily devotions. Would John Wesley have considered not taking his Bible on his preaching journeys, or would the early Methodist societies have gathered without reading or discussing the Word of God? Even Jesus quoted the prophets!

Why, then, the strong aversion to Bible study and scripture reading today? Why has Bible study in some congregations virtually gone out of style? Furthermore, why have people formed certain perceptions about different believers such as that United Methodists don't read or carry their Bibles and don't evangelize communities with the Word of God? Is it that we have moved so far away from our history that we no longer recognize it? I have had several conversations with staunch United Methodists about what United Methodists do and don't do. Here is a short list (see appendix A for the complete list):

- United Methodists don't go into communities to evangelize. Jehovah's Witnesses do.
- United Methodists don't shout in Sunday worship. Pentecostals do.
- United Methodists don't believe in spirit-filled, celebrative worship services. Baptists and Assemblies of God do.
- United Methodists only sing anthems.
- United Methodists don't believe in too much Bible study. The *Book of Discipline* is more important than the Bible.
- United Methodists don't, as a rule, carry their Bibles to church.

- United Methodists don't give testimonials about the Holy Spirit's working in their lives.
- United Methodists don't show joy or zeal in their praise and witness for Christ!

Although the above list of prevailing assumptions refers to United Methodists, perceptions of other denominations are just as ingrained in people's minds. Perhaps in looking at some United Methodist churches one could easily come to the above conclusions. However, such practices have not always characterized the spirit and temper of the Methodist movement.

If the above list is any indicator, it appears that everyone else is on fire but the United Methodists! This is highly paradoxical given that the early Methodist societies were known for their focus on preaching, Bible study, and revival. It is a shame that we have lost much of the evangelical fervor that contributed to the success of early Methodism. It is equally unfortunate that many churches have become ignorant of their own history and have moved away from stressing the fundamentals of Christian spirituality.

Moreover, attempts to recover basic precepts and practices are labeled and credited to other denominations who largely grew out of an evangelical "Great Awakening" begun largely by Methodists! Thus Bible study and Word-centeredness are avoided at all costs because people have become ashamed of such basic, mundane, frivolous, and superfluous expressions of religiosity. Such religious proprieties are too downright evangelical and simpleminded for the college educated, the sophisticated, and the professionally dedicated.

In short, we are embarrassed and ashamed by it all. We don't want to be seen carrying our Bibles because it's not in vogue. We don't want to make such an outward display of our spirituality because it is boastful. We feel too pretentious and too religious. What becomes of a people who are ashamed of their past and refuse to celebrate and retrieve those vital lessons of history that have contributed to their present success?

The philosopher George Santayana reminds us that "those who cannot remember the past are condemned to repeat it." Why must we apologize and justify our desire to go back to the Word of God, to teach and preach and live the Word of God? Why must we be defensive about establishing Word-centeredness, scriptural literacy, and revival traditions in our churches, and about challenging the people of God to study and read their Bibles so that the Word may become flesh in them?

This does not mean that laypeople and clergy must become Bible scholars, or that we must engage in the frivolous bombast of dousing people with spectacular litanies of Bible verses to demonstrate our Bible literacy. Neither does this mean that we must become spiritual voyeurs where every word we utter is punctuated by scripture, where we can't finish a sentence without profusely thanking and praising God! It is not that we shouldn't thank or praise God, but that the Word should take root in our lives so that our lives become a living text of the Word itself. It is not that we become Christ, but that we become Christlike by living according to his Word and its promises. As one preacher said, "It's not the text I preach but the text I live that makes the difference!"

How can it be that people have difficulty reading their Bibles in a time when the Bible is available in every form and format: on video and audio; in large and small print; a Bible for everyone, someone, and no one; a Bible for women, men, children, and youth; a Bible for the disgruntled and inflexible; a Bible for the hearing impaired and those running scared?

How is it that we can have people within the church who are leading others and are ignorant of the Word of

God? What does this say about the church? Are we a faith community of leaders and clergy oblivious to the Word of God? The Word is not valued, exalted, taught, or shared. How can a church grow spiritually if the Word is not revered and propagated, if the laity and clergy read *TV Guide* more than they read the Word of God? How can we serve and grow the church without the Word of God? Do we really believe that because we have attained higher education and are professionally trained we don't need those basic practices that engraft the Word of God on our lives? Incredibly, we get every other kind of training but Word of God training.

Every other discipline requires that students study, train, and then demonstrate what they have learned. Where, then, did we get the notion that we could become good stewards and Christians and avoid the diligent study of God's Word? Where did we ever get the idea that we could build viable churches for the long haul without stressing the centrality and power of the Bible? Many of us have lost our spiritual power because we have ignored the Bible as a power source in our lives. If the Word of God does not go forth and is not preached, taught, and instilled within the people of God, how shall God's kingdom flourish and prosper? Until we banish and ban scriptural illiteracy we will never realize our spiritual potential for kingdom building. Christian spirituality without the Bible is like flowers without sun, or a car without gas.

Word-centeredness essentially means the retrieval of a basic plan of scripture reading and daily devotion to give witness to the power and glory of God in our lives. The stress here is on basic, down-to-earth approaches to Christian spirituality that produce spiritual fruit in our kingdom labors. Word-centeredness means allowing the Word of God to take root in our lives so that the Word of God becomes a primary reference index for behavior and belief. This emphasis on the Word does not negate the importance and value of *reason, experience,* or *tradition.* It simply means that the Bible has a paramount place in the formation of Christian consciousness, value, and beliefs, and should be studied in order to grow in our witness, word, and wisdom. Such witness culminates in good biblical preaching and the development of a devotional life that is scripturally based and empowered.

Another important aspect of Word-centeredness from a Wesleyan tradition is that the study of scripture should lead to some apostolic engagement. This means moving beyond the confines of one's comfort zone, and compelling people to Christ. Bible study gives the believer confidence in standing on the Word and proclaiming that Word amid the solemn assemblies of the world. There is thus a blessed and certain assurance and conviction that urges the believer to tell someone about the love and goodness of Christ. Word-centeredness through Bible study does not simply mean individual edification, but the active translation of that witness into the larger community. In the case of Methodism, this zeal for the Word gave impetus and power to the early Methodist movement in a country that had become cloyed by the trite banalities of hierarchical, upper-class religiosity, and that is why it appealed so greatly to the plain people of England.

Simple, down-to-earth, practical applications of Christian spirituality compelled those "plain people" to view themselves not only as worthy recipients of God's power and grace, but active agents for kingdom building. Christianity therefore was not something simply for the rich and famous and powerful, but was placed within the grasp of the common man as Jesus intended.

Part of the evangelical inertia of many congregations may be ascribed, in part, to our failure to emphasize a

Wesleyan style of practicality in the things of Christ and church. Our organizational and theological complexity often belies and negates the simple rudiments of practical spirituality. Mainline seminaries seldom teach the fundamentals of Christian spirituality. Moreover, saving souls and reviving dead churches are scarcely topics of debate for either seminaries or the church.

Although times have changed, people have not changed all that much. The Word of God must still be preached and taught to souls languishing in the quagmires of consternation and despair! In order to develop viable models of spiritual empowerment we must go back to the basics. We must reclaim the Word of God as an axis power in our mission and ministry. We must shed the organizational and theological frivolities that prevent us from getting right down to the real nitty-gritty and reaching people where they are and where they hurt.

Getting Back to Basics:
Spiritual Training for Christian Leaders

Where did we ever get the idea that the Christian church could numerically grow without first growing spiritually? All numerical growth presupposes spiritual growth. Where did we get the idea that we can simply appoint people to leadership positions within the congregation but never develop a basic criteria for leadership? Most congregations create job descriptions that outline the criteria and qualifications needed for people holding Christian leadership positions in the church. We stress the importance of membership in the church, organizational skills, Christian experience, and other qualifications, but seldom cite the spiritual requirements for service. This results in leaders in key decision-making roles within the church and ministry who are not in spiritual formation, who do not read their Bibles or conduct daily devotions, and who do not pray or invoke the presence and power of the Holy Spirit in their lives or work. It is a small wonder that the church is plagued by a spiritual malaise and has floundered in the quagmires of membership decline for the past two decades.

Daniel Buttry puts it this way:

> The work of the the church, then, is to nurture spiritual growth, to help parent each of us in the process of becoming a fully mature disciple of Christ. Every member needs to be challenged to grow, for none of us can ever claim we have arrived. Too many churchgoers become complacent about spiritual growth. They feel what they learned as children in Sunday school is sufficient to last a lifetime.[16]

The great crime has been our failure to develop spiritual criteria for leaders and laity in the church. The church is a faith community, the Body of Christ, a spiritual entity, yet we make few spiritual requirements of those who lead others in ministry.

Establishing a Christian Training Academy

As a means of addressing the need for spiritually trained leaders, every church should institute a *back to basics program* or *spiritual boot camp of Christian training* where the fundamentals of Christian spirituality are taught. Often, denominationally sponsored training programs and workshops do not provide enough depth and are generally not contextually specific. Whereas many church training programs are theoretical and practically relevant, each church should also tailor its program to meet the needs of its constituents.

Unfortunately, many churches provide no spiritual training for their laypeople. How can the church truly qualify as a spiritual community when the leaders have not qualified themselves spiritually? Are we letting people off the hook by not requiring them to enroll in a back to basics program of Christian training? How can we develop a viable model of spiritual empowerment when the laity are not empowered spiritually to do the work of God?

The truth is we are not human beings having a spiritual experience, but spiritual beings having a human experience. Moreover, as a faith community, should not our primary focus be spiritual? Should we not offer programs of spiritual training that will equip the laity to lead according to the plan that God has prescribed for the people of God? One-time training programs are not enough. Christian training is a lifetime vocation. There is always something new to learn spiritually as we lead others in kingdom building.

A friend related his experience of hiking in the mountains. The original guide fell ill and a substitute was selected. The hike was a disaster. The substitute guide knew nothing about the mountain's terrain, the land, or the climate and conditions in which they were hiking. This guide was in a leadership position, but was not qualified to lead the expedition. In the end, a fellow hiker, who had more hiking experience, assumed the responsibilities of leading the group.

How can church leaders lead people on their journey to Christ when they are not acquainted with Christ, have no relationship with Christ, and cannot bear testimony to how far Christ has brought them? *We must stop the practice of just letting leaders fill in when they are not qualified to lead.* They should know something about the terrain on which they travel, the Word and promises of the Shepherd who leads them on the journey, and how to adapt to adverse conditions and help others through their storms. How can the spiritually blind lead others to spiritually high places when they cannot see where they are going?

What are the essential elements of a back to basics program? The following outlines some of the fundamental criteria needed to establish such a program (see appendix C for a detailed course outline).

1. **Spiritual formation and Christian training must become a priority as the foundation for church growth.** This means that existing and prospective church leaders must enroll in courses or programs that will strengthen them spiritually and amplify their understanding of what it means to be a Christian leader in the church.

2. **A standardized criteria of basic training must be developed that will empower the laity spiritually and equip them to faithfully lead the people of God.** Will these programs require Bible study of all leaders? What specific courses will equip leaders to facilitate the missional goals and objectives of a particular ministry? What important spiritual qualities should leaders exemplify in kingdom building and what programs will enable them to optimally attain such qualities? For example, course offerings through local church Christian training academies can range from *Conflict Resolution* to *Our Connectional Church* to the *Biblical Foundations of Church Leadership.*

3. **Human, material, and spiritual resources must be galvanized to establish a back to basics program in Christian spirituality.** Pastors must value such training programs for qualified laity. This type of support is critical because, sadly, some pastors sometimes do not want a spiritually empowered laity. As one clergyman remarked, "I don't want to give them too much training because they will

know what I know. If they know what I know, then they will want to be the pastor." In other words, pastors sometimes find spiritually qualified laity threatening to their role as chief shepherd. However, if trained properly, people can discern various gifts and graces. They recognize the value of *T.E.A.M.* or *Together Everyone Achieves More.* They can develop a greater appreciation of the pastor as chief shepherd of the flock and can faithfully support the ministry. In fact, spiritually empowered clergy and laity can develop a wholesome matrix of cointentional service to God's people that can empower everyone to be better leaders. Tensions invariably dissipate when clergy and laity realize the spiritual gifts they have in common, how those gifts can benefit the Body of Christ, and that they can become mutually empowered to build God's kingdom.

In establishing back to basics programs in Christian spiritual training in local congregations, we must be mindful of the following:

Profound realities are revealed in the simple things of life. *Simplifying the complex can elicit answers to the church's most perplexing problems.* Legendary coach Vince Lombardi of the Green Bay Packers once stated that when the team is losing it must go back to the fundamentals of the game. This means that however professional the team becomes, it cannot obtain the desired results without executing the elementary principles of blocking, tackling, running, and throwing. Such basics are often taken for granted by professionals, but it is precisely such skills that need further honing to achieve true excellence.

These same truths apply to the church. Perhaps we

have become so professional in our orientation to the vocation of ministry and ecclesia that we have failed to execute the fundamentals that bring people to Christ. Our calling people unto Christ means that we must go back to those Christian basics that are essential to the church's future growth and prosperity.

For example, where would The United Methodist Church be now if the early Methodists had not done simple, basic things like witnessing to the unchurched and unsaved, reading their Bibles, forming small societies, meeting in the homes of laypeople, reaching out to the poor and oppressed, praying, fasting, tithing, and serving those in need of the good news of the gospel? Could The United Methodist Church and other mainline Protestant denominations have arrived at a point of strength without doing the simple things that compel folk to Christ?

Manfred Marquardt tells us that John and Charles Wesley established small medical clinics that dispensed pharmaceuticals to the sick and provided loans to the poor—simple things that reached people on the grounds of their ultimate needs. Ministry was to body and soul and was done with head and heart.[17]

We need to train our leaders in the basics of Christian spirituality, discipleship, and stewardship to strengthen and grow our churches. By not stressing the importance of Bible study, developing strong devotional lives, and actively engaging in programs that nurture spiritual growth, the church will continue to decline because it has failed to grow and minister in God's way.

Cultivating an Ethos of Gifting

Developing a Spiritual Gifts Ministry

Christ expects us to bear fruit in our ministries (Matt. 7:15-20). Spiritual gifts germinate spiritual fruit. If gifts are developed then fruit should become manifest. If gifts are not nurtured then the ministry can bear little or no fruit. A number of churches have withered on the vine because they have failed to cultivate an ethos of spiritual gifting. This means developing a climate where spiritual gifts can be *explored, discovered, claimed, nurtured,* and *shared.* The soil must therefore be tilled and the conditions must be developed that will allow for the manifestation of all spiritual gifts in ministry. Paul exhorts us to develop spiritual gifts that will build up the church (1 Cor. 14:12). There are many gifts and God has blessed us all with at least one gift (1 Cor. 12:1-11).

Developing an ethos of gifting means that the church must create a context for the possible emergence of all gifts. This means spiritual gifts, as well as the gifts of God, which include *faith* (Eph. 2:8; Phil. 1:29), *repentance* (Acts 11:18), *wisdom* (Prov. 2:6; James 1:5), and *grace* (Ps. 84:11; James 4:6). Furthermore, spiritual and material gifts are blessings from God. If a congregation prioritizes the development of spiritual gifts, God can bless the church with material growth. Material prosperity can flow from spiritual prosperity because we are doing it God's way.

There are other gifts as well, but unfortunately, some denominations favor specific types of gifts more than others. I have wondered why in The United Methodist Church and in some other denominations there is only nominal emphasis on the gifts of the Holy Spirit—such as the gifts of tongues, interpretation of tongues, healing, miracles, and of wisdom and discernment. In many instances, preaching, teaching, or evangelizing are not referred to as gifts.

Why are these gifts seldom recognized and celebrated in the church? Why don't we discuss, cultivate, or celebrate them? Denominational and church leaders often refer to the "gifts and graces" of individuals, but seldom do we see the power of these gifts actualized in local churches or district or regional meetings. Unfortunately, most of these types of gatherings are preoccupied with transforming church structures and passing social legislation. What happened to the celebration and uplift of spiritual gifts as empowerment for ministry? Why don't bishops and other prelates of the church have conferences where spiritual gifts can be recognized, celebrated, and deployed in the Body of Christ? Shouldn't these meetings also be altar calls for healing and empowering pastors and laypeople?

Several ministers lamented the closing of a United Methodist church and the purchase of the building by another denomination. The ministry in the new church is now growing and thriving. "Why couldn't we do the same thing? What's the difference between them and us?" asked one. "They believe in miracles and we don't," said the other. "They believe in, welcome, and practice the use of all gifts of the Holy Spirit! We believe only in some gifts."

What happened to the gifts of miracles and healing? Did they stop with the apostolic age? I was reprimanded by a member of the congregation after we conducted our first healing service at Hope Church. "Where did you get the service?" she asked sharply. "From the *United Methodist Book of Worship*," I replied. This staunch United Methodist did not even know that healing services were a part of Methodist tradition. We have so distanced ourselves from such practices that we don't even know what is part of our tradition anymore. Donald W. Dayton has done extensive work in uncovering the Methodist roots of Pentecostalism and other evangelical movements. His discussion of Wesley's stress on bearing spiritual fruit may surprise those who have negated or omitted the Wesleyan apostolic imperatives.[18]

If the church intentionally develops an environment where spiritual gifts and gifting are allowed to flourish, it can set the stage for new evangelical fervor and power that can rescue the church from its current malaise. Structural changes and strategies only nominally effect renewal in the church. You can change church structures all you want, but if attitudes are not changed and souls are not converted and set on fire for Christ it becomes business as usual. Nothing really changes because the people have not experienced genuine transformation of their hearts and spirits. Congregations, as well as main-line denominations, need a whole new outlook and orientation toward the cultivation of spiritual gifts and graces to empower local congregations to be in vital ministry to others.

Every church should actively promote spiritual gifting. After all, does God not work to bless the church through various gifts and graces? Churches should prioritize spiritual gifts as a foundation of spiritual growth and vitality, encourage people to discover and develop gifts for the glory of God and kingdom building, and offer opportunities for people to learn more about spiritual gifts and the meaning and process of gifting as forms of spiritual empowerment.

There was a time when herbal medicine, homeopathic, and naturopathic healing were the only forms of medicine. As the medical profession cultivated more scientific and empirical healing methods and therapies, the homeopathic approaches were denigrated as quackery and were eventually displaced by new paradigms. Thus the old nutritional paradigms for healing were supplanted by modern scientific models. But the medical establishment forgot that many of those nutritional approaches actually worked to make people well. Now that naturalistic and nutritional therapies are making a comeback in the medical market, they have achieved the status of alternative medicine. We no longer refer to chiropractic or naturopathy as quackery because many of their healing methods have proved themselves to be safe and viable over time. Now as the medical establishment reevaluates healing therapies and techniques, many of these alternative approaches are being taught in medical schools and are once again affirmed by some segments of the mainstream medical establishment as viable methods of healing.

Perhaps mainline Protestant denominations have developed the same attitude toward the more charismatic, evangelical gifts of the spirit as the modern medical establishment long held for naturopathic healing. Such spiritual gifts are now regarded as forms of sorcery because their efficacy cannot be scientifically or empirically proved. Perhaps this is precisely the antidote the church needs to heal itself from its present sickness. What was once mainstream has now become alternative. What is now alternative should, perhaps, become once again mainstream.

So the question now becomes: Why do we as a church keep doing the same old things the same old way? Why do we emphasize the same old practices that do not get the optimum results? Why doesn't the church nurture the more charismatic gifts? Perhaps we need to reexamine and relegitimize these alternative approaches to spirituality and incorporate them into the working theologies of local congregations.

The true church is a place where all gifts can be realized and manifested. In order for the church to realize its true spiritual potential and become empowered spiritually, all gifts must be cultivated and nurtured to provide fruit for ministry. These gifts cannot be conjured. Only God determines when and where God's gifts will be made manifest. All spiritual gifts are used for building up and edifying others in Christ.

However, if the Holy Spirit is welcomed and celebrated, a context in which all gifts can be realized will be created.

In addition, the more charismatic gifts, such as the gift of healing, need to be nurtured and grown in our churches. And why not? Isn't God still in the business of healing broken and shattered lives? How many times have we seen God heal cancer and other maladies after the doctors have given up? Is God not still in charge? Why, then, don't we emphasize these gifts more as a basis of spiritual empowerment in our churches?

The church needs to cultivate an ethos of spiritual gifting where gifts are unapologetically, unabashedly, and unashamedly developed, shared, and celebrated in the life of local congregations. Until the church affirms the importance of spiritual gifting and actively promotes it through mission and ministry, it will scarcely attain its true spiritual vitality and power. It may never maximize its spiritual potential because it has devalued the importance of spiritual gifting.

Strengthening Your Vertical Connection

The United Methodist Church, which is similar to several other denominations, is a connectional church where congregations are vitally linked into a common bond of faith, tradition, and praxis. We stress the importance of being in connection with one another, which is a great strength of the church. However, this connection is one of a horizontal nature, where organizations and institutions within the church strengthen their ties by consolidating the church's mission around common goals and objectives. For many of us, we live in a community and are part of a denomination that values the importance of being in connection, but in our striving for stronger bonds and ties, do we forget the importance of our vertical connection to Christ? In an effort to fortify our organizational structures are we solidifying our faith? Are we growing spiritually? Are we clarifying our relationship with the God who has called us into being and ministry?

A story from the *Upper Room* captures this dilemma. A man went on a camping trip, heard of an approaching storm, and began feverishly pitching his tent. When he finished his work, he got into his tent. The storm came and blew the tent away. The man recalled that in his fervor to build this shelter from the storm, "I lengthened my cords but I failed to strengthen my stakes."[19]

As a church, is our problem that our approach to things is always so horizontal that we fail to dig in vertically to give us true anchoring for the storm now raging? The church cannot afford to lengthen its cords horizontally and yet fail to strengthen its faith vertically. We need to affirm ourselves horizontally in community, but we must first understand that we are called to be a spiritual community—a people of faith and vitality who bear witness to the continuing revelation of Christ in our lives. This means that we are vertically connected. The horizontal and vertical tension that exists in us and in the church signifies our cross, the parenthesis of our spiritual striving.

For example, in my denomination we often speak of appointing pastors to churches and appointing leaders for service in the church. The appointment is wonderful, but what is the appointment without the anointing? Why do we never make reference to anointing or being anointed for service in the church? Why is our stress always so horizontal that the vertical dimensions of our calling and being are virtually unspoken or obscured? By referring to ministry as a profession there is a whole constellation of assumptions that are horizontal in nature, which virtually obfuscate the vertical, spiritual, anointing of our calling to Christ. Perhaps our failure to emphasize ministry as a higher spiritual calling and that God anoints persons for service in the church is one reason why so many congregations flounder and perish.

Anointing presupposes an outpouring from above from God. Perhaps, as pastors, we have lost that sense of belief in the vertical that has undermined our spiritual power and authority in ministry. By retrieving the language of holiness, developing Word-centered churches, emphasizing spiritual training, cultivating an ethos of gifting, and renewing our vertical connection, we can reestablish an intimate relationship with Christ that will ultimately empower the church to grow. These elements are indispensable to developing models of spiritual empowerment in local congregations as well as the larger denomination.

Summary Questions

1. Is the Holy Spirit invited to anoint, guide, and direct your church's ministry?
2. Does your congregation practice sanctification and holiness as part of the church's mission and ministry?
3. Are parishioners comfortable using spiritual language in your church? If not, why?
4. Is salvation and saving souls a missional priority in the church? If not, why?
5. Do you invite persons into Christ after the proclamation in your worship experience?
6. Does your congregation stress the importance of being born again?
7. Does your congregation stress the importance of having a conversion experience?
8. Is reconversion or renewal of membership vows or a recommitment to Christ encouraged in your church?

9. Has your church ever conducted a service of corporate worship for confession, repentance, and forgiveness?

10. Does a spirit of revival permeate the mission and ministries of your church?

11. Is the church joyful, praise oriented, and celebrative?

12. Does your church stress the foundational principles for spiritual empowerment, such as developing a prayer life, Bible study, devotion, and other spiritual disciplines?

13. Do parishioners bring their Bibles to church? Are Bible studies offered in your church?

14. Do people in your church attend Bible study? What percentage of your Bible study is comprised of church members, constituents, and nonmembers?

15. Does your church have a basic program of spiritual training for leaders and laity that educates them in the fundamentals of Christian spiritual leadership?

16. Have any of your current leaders spiritually qualified themselves to lead in the church? Have they had any basic training for service in your church?

17. What is your current criteria for leadership selection in the church?

18. Do you have a Christian training academy?

19. Is the discovery and use of spiritual gifts encouraged in your church?

20. Does your church offer programs that enable parishioners to discover and cultivate spiritual gifts?

21. Do you offer courses on discovering spiritual gifts? Do you conduct spiritual gifts inventories for new and longtime members?

22. What are the predominant gifts manifested in your church?
23. Is your church a place where all spiritual gifts have the potential for being manifested?
24. Does your church have a vertical or higher spiritual sense of its mission and ministry? Explain.
25. What current obstacles are preventing you from establishing models of spiritual empowerment for your church?
26. What steps can be taken to develop models of spiritual empowerment in your church as prescribed in the foregoing chapter?

Summary Checklist

☐ Convene parishioners to dialogue about your denomination's holiness traditions and how such traditions can be incorporated into the life of the church today.

☐ Create programs and opportunities to discuss and encourage using the language of holiness in the life of the church. Help people understand the tradition of holiness from a denominational (e.g., Wesleyan United Methodist) perspective.

☐ Prioritize saving souls and salvation as part of the church's mission and ministry. Shape your ministry around these issues by instituting a hymn of invitation after the proclamation, and developing discipleship and outreach ministries around this priority.

☐ Conduct a healing or service of confession, repentance, and forgiveness for the church so as to eradicate the barriers to spiritual progress.

☐ Create a variety of back to basics Bible studies that will spiritually empower people to build their spiritual lives, and seek ways to encourage people to attend. Help the congregation obtain a sense of the importance of studying, believing, and practicing God's Word.

☐ Convene a Christian training committee and develop a Christian training academy that offers a variety of courses on spiritual formation that will empower people to lead spiritually in the church.

☐ Establish a spiritual gifts ministry. Teach courses on discovering spiritual gifts. Conduct a spiritual gifts inventory for all parishioners in the church.

☐ Match spiritual gifts with specific ministries for the overall empowerment of the church.

☐ Encourage the development and use of all spiritual gifts. Offer courses, seminars, or workshops on gifting, and empower people to discover and use their gifts for God's glory.

CHAPTER THREE

Clergy Empowerment: To Be Seers, Builders, and Leaders of God's People

Claiming Your Spiritual Authority

In some churches, pastors seem to be viewed as managers or caretakers of a particular parish. They go to a church, do as they are told, and sit quietly and patiently until they move to their next church. In such cases, pastors simply bide their time, seldom challenging the people of God spiritually or moving the church into new spiritual frontiers.

However, pastors are not called to be idlers, politicians, and managers of churches. They are called to be leaders. Craig Hickman presents a cogent model that affirms the need for pastors as both leaders and managers.[1] The two styles of leadership need not exclude each other. One can have the mind of a manager and the soul and compassion of a leader. The manager analyzes and organizes the church for ministry, whereas the leader provides vision, direction, and impetus for building the church's future. Soul force and mind force can come together into one potent force for positive change. All too frequently in the institutional and bureaucratic church, pastors become managers who maintain order and conform to the status quo, as opposed to leaders who transform and change the church positively for the future. If the church is to be empowered to grow spiritually and to revitalize itself for the future, it must have pastors who will be leaders and who will claim their spiritual authority as servants of the Lord.

Just as businesses cannot maintain or manage themselves into profitability, churches cannot manage themselves into growth. In 1998, approximately seventy churches in and around Detroit never baptized or saved a single soul for service. In business, this is equivalent to seventy dealerships of the Ford Motor Company not selling a single car in 1998. If this trend continued, the business would go out of business. Likewise, some churches have had to go out of business because of the failure of the clergy and laity to challenge, inspire, and lead the people of God into the future.

Pastors must therefore equip themselves to lead and must claim their spiritual calling and authority as servants of God. The church is more than a business or organization. It is a living organism capable of dynamic, progressive change. Clergy must have foresight, wisdom, courage, and strength. We must have a higher sense of our calling as God's servants and feel spiritually empowered to help build the church's future. Men and women of God must see themselves as more than managers or caretakers of God's kingdom, and must not become puppets, but pastors. Being a true pastor means cultivating leadership abilities and skills. It means standing in the fray of battle and having the courage to make those decisions that will positively empower the church's future.

By going back to spiritual basics pastors can reclaim spiritual authority, which for clergy is important in revitalizing and empowering the church spiritually. How will the pastor ever become truly effective in leading God's people if he or she does not have a higher sense of spiritual calling and ethereal purpose, or does not stand spiritually upon the authority God has granted him or her to lead the people? Thus, knowing who you are and whose you are as a child of God will help in establishing your place in ministry among the people you are called to lead and serve. Clergy develop a true identity and a firm foundation for ministry by looking to God as a source of spiritual power and strength. Establishing and reclaiming spiritual authority for leadership in the church necessitates the cultivation of a living dialogical relationship with Christ. Claim your spiritual authority by nurturing your relationship with Christ through prayer, service, and the study of God's word.

Discover Your Spiritual Gifts

Do you know your true gifts for ministry? Are you aware of your strengths and limitations as a pastor? In the areas where you are not so strong have you selected laity or other clergy to take up the slack? Do you have gifts that are commensurate and compatible with ministry?

A central deterrent to healthy and vital churches for some denominations is *spiritual mismatching*. Congregations and clergy both have spiritual gifts. It is true that clergy and congregations with different gifts can complement each other, but if a church has a particular profile of leadership that has been essential to its growth, it is important to find clergy to match that profile.

One way to assess if a pastor and congregation are an appropriate fit for each other in ministry is through a gifts workshop and inventory. It is also important for clergy to understand their gifts and graces for ministry and to actively grow and nurture those gifts. It is not enough to simply say, "God called me and I went." Would God call servants to ministry without equipping them with spiritual gifts for effective service? Has God simply developed the most gifted leaders for the secular community and the world of business?

Gifted leaders are also needed within the church to serve God's people, build the church, and promote the Kingdom. Pastors must inventory their gifts and work to develop those gifts for which they have promise and potential. *Spiritual gifts lead to spiritual fruit in ministry.* It is important that the church take seriously the importance of inventorying and evaluating spiritual gifts as a foundation for empowering the church spiritually for future ministry.

Is It Well with Your Soul?

Howard Thurman was famous for posing this question to clergy: "How is it with *your* soul?" In a profession where we are called to give and serve, clergy often make the mistake of not taking good care of their bodies and souls. Often, we, in the words of Henri Nouwen, find ourselves as "wounded healers," in need of a balm of Gilead to heal our sin-sick souls.

No other profession requires so much of persons as ministry. Pastors must wear many different hats and be many things to many different people. There is enormous pressure to succeed, to win souls, to present a clean wholesome image, and to merit the confidence of the people we serve. We must often present this image to our own detriment.

Some clergy have developed unrealistic and unhealthy leadership modalities and lifestyles that precipitate burnout and depression. They have developed what my mentor, Philip Harley, calls the *Messiah Complex.*[2] In leading the people we have messianic expectations of Christ and ourselves as servants of Christ, and there is nothing more disconcerting than a broken-down, burned-out messiah. In the effort to be all things to all people, we destroy our health and undermine our own spiritual well-being.

As pastors, it is important to develop strong and consistent devotional and prayer lives, spend time with our families, and cultivate recreational outlets that we enjoy; for how can we adequately serve the people of God when we are "all messed up"? If our parishioners are to get well, we must personify wellness, health, and vitality. As pastors, we must realize that it is OK for us to take care of ourselves. It is OK to meet our own needs and do some things that we enjoy doing; or as my grandfather admonished his spiritual son, Joseph Roberts, Sr., pastor at Ebenezer Baptist Church in Atlanta, Georgia, "Discretion is the better part of valor, and never wear muddy shoes in your own house." Don't feel guilty for wanting to have a good time. Don't apologize if you want to play golf, go bowling or fishing, or go to the ballpark. Have some clean wholesome fun! Enjoy yourself! Get the crick out of your neck, the lump out of your back, and get well! Live! Make it well with your soul! Loosen up and liven up!

Developing and Implementing a Vision Plan for Your Church

Vision simply means imaging new possibilities for the future. Therefore, your vision for the church is living dreams you hope will become reality. Unfortunately, too few churches have a vision plan for the future. Too often congregations expect the larger denominational church to articulate and implement their vision for them. Although the denomination has a vision for the larger church, each church should have a vision for itself in relation to the local community that it is called to serve.

Cultivating a vision for the church's future should be based on many things, including: the history and traditions of the Christian church and the denomination; prayer, personal experience, age, race, and culture; the Bible; social, political, economic, and technological trends; and the needs of congregation and community. Most important though is the leadership and guidance of the Holy Spirit.

Although a vision for the church will grow out of the past, it will also raise expectations about the church's future prospects and possibilities. A vision should always speak to the specific needs of people and prepare them for the future.

Many pastors carry a vision in their heads of what they would like to see the church become in the future. Regrettably, few write that vision down and share it with their congregations for implementation. A carefully crafted, written vision plan is critical for every church. This vision for the church does not grow out of the pastor's mind alone, but emerges from his or her dialogue with various members of the congregation and the community.

Sometimes pastors and churches resist creating a written vision because of the possibility of a leadership change. However, this does not have to pose a stumbling block to the the development and implementation of a church's vision plans. If every pastor and congregation developed and adopted a vision plan for the church's future, that vision could already be in place when the next pastor arrives. The vision's success need not be predicated on whether a certain pastor serves a church. The vision or strategic plan can continue regardless of a change in pastoral appointment.

It is vital that pastors have, share, and implement a five-year strategic plan or vision plan for local churches. Each church should develop a vision or dream team whose sole purpose is to discuss, plan, and implement the church's vision for the future.[3] "Where there is no vision, the people perish" (Prov. 29:18 KJV). This team need not be comprised only of members of the church. It might also include business and civic leaders from the community or other resource persons who can imagine and project a viable future for the church.

For example, this vision team could spend up to a year discussing, developing, and evaluating a vision based on the needs and aspirations of the church and community. Initially, the team might conduct a survey of the church and community, and then begin discussion about developing a strategic plan. Such a plan would include *who we are, why we are, where we are, how we are, where we hope to go,* and *how and when we plan to get there.* Appendix B includes vision inventory questions that can help guide churches through the visioning process.

Sometimes churches assume that because they are doing God's work there is no need to plan for the future because God will take care of everything. This thinking creates false perceptions about what is expected of a faith community. God does not work solely through spontaneity. In looking at creation, one can see that God developed a blueprint for the imprint of creation. There is a rational order and substance to creation. To say that the church should not develop a strategic plan for the future is irresponsible, and thinking that the Holy Spirit is without order and purpose is equally problematic.

Some churches cannot grow because pastors and laity have not developed and implemented a viable vision for the future. They are like ships on the seas with no particular destination and engage in what James MacGregor Burns called the "politics of drift." They are drifting nowhere and are going nowhere. Time and resources are being wasted because no one has a clear vision for the future.

God will reveal God's vision to the pastor and laity of that church if they are in tune with the Lord and are obedient servants. The vision, then, is not simply what the pastors or laity desire for the church's future, but is a vision that God has for that congregation, which is revealed through its clergy and parishioners.

In looking at the Bible we see that God's vision for God's people is revealed through certain individuals. The vision of Israel's greatness did not simply grow out of the minds of the people, but was cultivated in their covenantal relationship. Because they had a viable relationship with Yahweh, they knew that Yahweh had great expectations and high hopes for them. They knew that they were special and chosen for a specific purpose. They were convinced that God had called them, that God was on their side, and that God would give them victory over their adversaries.

The same is true in the New Covenant. God does not want the church to flounder and perish. God has a great vision for the people. The people must catch sight of that vision and live according to its promises. Catching sight of God's vision for the church presupposes a genuine, dialogical relationship with God. It means being intimately and spiritually related to God. How can the people of God ever know God's vision for them if they never talk to the Lord, never cultivate a living relationship to know what God expects of them?

The idea of pastoral vision is rooted in the understanding that the pastor is walking and talking with God, for if the people of God implement God's vision God's way, they can enjoy the fruits of spiritual success. Could our failure to develop a viable vision be due to the fact that we are not in relationship with Christ and do not consult him enough to know what he wants for us, and thereby we experience decline and inertia in our ministries?

What is God's vision for your church? How will you enable people to see that vision and carry it out? These questions revert back to the importance of spiritual training and being open to the direction of the Holy Ghost. If the people are of one spiritual accord, centered in God's Word and obedient to God's will, God's vision for the church's future is achievable. Encouraging people to buy into the vision need not be a calamity or a struggle. If we are truly a faith community, in genuine relationship with Christ, then we should have some idea of what Christ expects of us. We should have some notion of how to do ministry and how to empower others to Christ. Those who are in a genuine dialogical relationship should not be in perpetual debate or struggle about what God wants for their future.

What Visions Do

Visions inherently raise expectations about the future, help people invest in the future, consolidate interests, promulgate and solidify values, energize people, galvanize cooperative networks essential to community and faith building, and enable people to share their faith and beliefs by building community around common ideals. They encourage the flow of creative and innovative ideas, facilitate dialogue about the church's future, cultivate and nurture people, clarify dreams and aspirations, provide a blueprint for the future, help people navigate through the chaos and doldrums of the status quo, and create opportunities for service that will benefit people.

- Visions challenge, empower, inspire, grow, create, uplift, renew, and restore the people of God. Visions renew and energize congregations for the future.

- Visions grow from needs, aspirations, purpose, imagination, faith, and mission. Visions are reality based.

- Visions require faith, motivation, dedication, cooperation, trust, mutual relationships, innovation, perspiration, implementation, and evaluation to succeed. Visions require hard work.

- Visions are cultivated and sustained through faith, courage, prayer, creativity, conviction, perseverance, caring, sharing, and the guidance of the Holy Spirit.

- Visions build and sustain community and create a sense of empowerment, ownership, and investment among God's people.

- Visions, after they have been incubated and implemented, take on a life of their own and benefit a much greater number of people than their originators.

Remember that the work of early Christians and Methodists began from visionaries such as Jesus Christ, the early apostles, John Wesley, Francis Asbury, Philip Otterbein, Richard Allen, and Jacob Albright. *Pastors must also be visionaries who lead the church into the future.*

Establishing Your Moral Authority

Establishing moral authority is important in spiritually empowering congregations for the future. Although we are all sinners, it is highly important that the pastor establish moral authority for leadership among God's people. How can the pastor effectively lead and grow the church if he or she cannot be trusted or believed, or is one in whom the people cannot invest confidence and faith? How can the pastor cultivate moral authority when he or she is violating every moral and ethical code in the book? Some pastors admonish their congregations: "Do as I say and not as I do." This cripples the church and kills the confidence of parishioners. Clergy should be showing people a way into God's salvation, mercy, and grace—not giving them a way out.

Among black preachers in particular, stories are told of the sexual dalliances and moral misadventures of various clergy. Unfortunately, within some black churches a culture of acceptance of such indiscretions is tolerated as long as "the negro can preach." The assumption is if a pastor is caught in wrongdoing and cannot preach the Word, he creates a double jeopardy. However, if he can preach the Word with fire and authority, the congregation may forgive him for his sins. (I intentionally use the word *him* because a kind of hypocrisy related to clergywomen exists in this area. If a female preacher were accused of sexual impropriety and could preach a mighty Word, would the same courtesies and forgiveness be extended to her? I don't think so!)

The problem is one of the erosion of moral authority. How can a spiritual leader have the confidence of the people when he or she is engaged in doublespeak by lying to his or her parishioners and deceitfully engaging in religious roulette? America and the ministry profession have been greatly damaged by mainstream religious leaders whose moral faux pas have cast a giant shadow on the entire profession of ministry.

Now, more than ever, the church needs moral rectitude among leaders and laity. The devil undoubtedly has a field day with our moral depravity and will use it as an instrument to demolish the church. Practice what you preach, and preach what you practice. This will go a long way in winning the confidence and respect of the people you serve.

Keeping Your Eyes on the Prize

It is important that clergy keep their eyes on the prize when serving God's people. Many pastors are consumed by the minutiae of ministry and can easily lose sight of their fundamental purpose for ministry. Because many clergy lead smaller churches where the demands for mastering the details of multiple ministries is often overwhelming, one can easily overlook the fundamental purpose for being in service. It is therefore important that pastors keep their eyes on the prize and prioritize what is important in their ministries.

Many clergy become so consumed by the daily rounds of ministries that they have no adequate time for weekly sermon preparation. A primary function of the pastor is to preach the Word of God in season and out of season, and to take the necessary time for devotion and study to bring a fresh Word each week. However, if the pastor is immersed in administration, pastoral care, and other important and superfluous concerns in ministry, finding time to prepare for sermons can be a problem.

Keeping your eyes on the prize means staying focused on your primary reason for being in ministry, which is to preach, teach, and reach persons for Christ. The higher calling of ministry should be a primary focus of concern as you meet the needs of the people you serve. Do not become distracted by the unnecessary things that consume your energy and drain your strength so that you do not have the time and strength to tend to the things that really matter. Keeping your spiritual focus on Christ through conflict, storms, and the other challenges of ministry will help create an anchor for effective ministry over the long haul.

Summary Questions

1. Do you have spiritual authority in your leadership of God's people? Do parishioners understand your role as spiritual guide, director, and leader? How have you helped them interpret and understand your role as spiritual leader of your congregation?

2. Do you have gifts for ministry? Have you personally conducted a spiritual gifts inventory? How are you using those gifts to empower yourself for ministry and to empower those you are called to serve? Do you possess gifts for ministry that you are not using in your ministry? What are those gifts and why are you not using them? Name and list your gifts.

3. Do you feel spiritually empowered to lead God's people?

4. Does your church recognize, celebrate, and appreciate your gifts for ministry?

5. Is it well with your soul, as shepherd of God's sheep? Do you regularly conduct devotions, prayer, and Bible study for the uplift and nurture of your own soul? How often do you take vacation? Do you work during those vacations? Do you feel fatigue, burnout, or frustration in ministry? Why? If so, how will you remedy these problems?

6. Do you take time off for rest, relaxation, and time with your family? How often?

7. Do you have a vision for your church? Have you received input on that vision from members of the church? Have they bought into the vision? Have you written that vision down and disseminated it with the larger church? Does your church have a three- to five-year vision or strategic plan? Have you convened a vision or dream team?

8. Are you committed to dig in, serve, build, and grow your present church, or are you already looking to leave before you have begun? Why? What are the factors compelling your desire to leave your present church?

9. Do you recognize, celebrate, and empower the gifts of laity in your church? If not, why not? If so, how?

10. What moral climate has been created in your church as a result of your leadership? Do you have moral authority in the church? Do the people respect your leadership? Are you walking the talk?

11. What is your clergy leadership style? Charismatic? Managerial? Visionary? Functional? Facilitative? Autocratic? How is this style conducive to the spiritual and numerical growth of your congregation?

12. How do you handle conflict with parishioners? Do you personally model a style of conflict resolution that is worthy of emulation by parishioners?

Summary Checklist

☐ Develop your personal devotional and prayer life to strengthen you for ministry.

☐ Regularly take time off for rest, relaxation, and rejuvenation for your own well-being and that of your family.

☐ Discover and inventory your spiritual gifts and cultivate them for service in God's church.

☐ Encourage others to discover and utilize their gifts for kingdom building.

☐ Choose and convene a vision or dream team. Develop and write a three- to five-year vision plan for your church. This plan will cover all of the ministry and service areas of the church. What would you like to see these ministry areas achieve in the next three to five years? How will you mobilize resources to set goals and objectives to achieve this vision? Disseminate the vision to the larger congregation and solicit their input. Conduct an evaluation of the vision and its effectiveness.

☐ Claim your spiritual power and moral authority as a servant of God.

☐ Practice what you preach and build where you are.

CHAPTER FOUR

Lay Empowerment: To Be Hearers, Believers, and Doers of God's Word

Becoming Followers of the Way and Using Your Gifts for God's Glory

If the laity are scripturally illiterate and are not Word-centered, biblically based, and Holy Ghost-directed in their orientation to service, the church can stagnate and stunt its growth potential. Laity must also be encouraged to discover and use their gifts for God's glory. My personal mission statement is *show people God's way, and stay out of God's way.* This means that clergy and laity, as servants of God, should strive to be followers *of* the way and not followers *in* the way. This also means that as people of God we should point people in the direction that they should go, but avoid selfish inclinations that often put us out of sync with the will of God. Both clergy and laity should work closely and covenantally to facilitate spiritual empowerment and growth.

Often people with great potential are discouraged from serving the church because selfish pastors or spiritually insecure leaders impede their progress and stifle their participation in the Body of Christ. There are many examples of clergy who preach people into the church only to have the laity chase those same people out. An often heard phrase is, "The preacher can preach them in, but the laity must keep them in." On the other hand, there are also many examples of insecure, parochial, and myopic clergy who are threatened by gifted laypeople and thereby discourage them from kingdom building.

In addition, too many male clergy are threatened by dynamic, gifted, and progressive female clergy. This is especially true in some black churches. Women are still subordinated, devalued, and negated for service, and some are viewed as being unworthy to set foot in the pulpit. Sometimes it is congregations who are wary of women preachers, with much of the animus coming from other women who dislike women pastors. However, if the church is to be empowered it must create an environment where all people can use their gifts for the glory of God. Both clergy and laity must strive to develop an ethos where *all* people can grow and develop their potential for service.

Encouraging others to serve by creating an atmosphere where failure is not fatal is an important hallmark of empowered laity. The black church is one of the few places where you can sing off-key, forget a line in a play, mispronounce words from the pulpit and pew, and still be affirmed as a child of God. The black church provided (and continues to provide) an environment where people could develop their gifts without condemnation or ridicule. How does the church cultivate such an environment for service?

1. Pastors and laypeople must recognize that the church does not ultimately belong to them, but to God. Therefore, our tenure of caretaking and stewardship is very short and we must empower others, who will build up the church and ensure its future, with the necessary gifts and graces.

Clergy and laity must see themselves as people of God, the Body of Christ, whom God has called and gifted to lead and serve cooperatively and not competitively in all areas of the church's ministry. We are all followers of Christ who are commissioned to build and serve his church. This means both laity and clergy must have a vertical connection in their calling to serve Christ, and must understand God's way of doing things in kingdom building. For example, it is the devil's way to keep the gifted of God out of the church and to fight with the weapons of the world. However, God's way opens the door to those who are gifted, and encourages and upholds believers in the faith rather than belittling, discouraging, and destroying them.

2. Clergy and laity must develop a strong spiritual and devotional life through prayer and Bible study, and must live Christ-centered lives. Christ-centered means using Christ and the guidance of the Holy Spirit as the ultimate reference point for conduct and belief. It means having reverence for God, obedience to Christ, and a willingness to selflessly serve in ministry. Also, it posits putting on the mind of Christ, evaluating things as Christ would, and asking ourselves two fundamental questions: *What would Jesus do? What would Jesus have me do?*

3. Laypeople must respect the office of clergy and recognize that clergy are called and anointed to shepherd and lead local churches. Conversely, pastors must respect the office of laity and empower them to serve.

4. Churches must find ways of facilitating ministry by being part of the solutions and not part of the problems of ministry. Ministry should be potential-based and problem solving.

5. Congregations must have an attitude of agape and philia, love and service, to God's people and support the ministry by prayers, presence, gifts, and service.

These are the elements of spiritual empowerment that can enable laity and clergy to covenant the church's revitalization for the future.

Qualifying to Lead Spiritually and Modeling Christian Spirituality

In order to faithfully model true Christian spirituality, laity must spiritually qualify themselves to be leaders in God's church. Appendix E provides a basic outline for how to live a Christian life. These precepts are the basis of Christian faith and praxis that can help laypeople deepen their spirituality. As chapter 2 details, by going back to basics we can develop models of spirituality that are consistent with God's Word and can elicit positive growth.

Many churches flounder because they are not training leaders God's way. Numerous churches are undergoing leadership crises where laity are not equipped to provide the proper leadership in kingdom building. Criteria other than membership must be implemented if churches are to be spiritually revitalized. How can God be pleased with churches when people are allowed to serve and lead and have not qualified for such important leadership positions?

Developing a Consistent Devotional Life

Spiritual formation is a lifetime process. Each church leader should be actively engaged in spiritual formation and development. Many leaders do not have consistent and regular devotional lives. Often they think attending Sunday school as a child is sufficient training for church leadership. They do not read their Bibles and they do not pray.

If the church is to be empowered spiritually, laity and clergy must develop strong devotional lives by reading their Bibles, praying, fasting, and devoting themselves to spiritual formation and empowerment. They must learn to tarry in the spirit, invoke the presence and power of the Holy Ghost, discover and activate spiritual gifts for service, and submit themselves to the leadership of the Father, Son, and Holy Ghost for service in the church. They must translate that power of witness into the larger community for the transformation and uplift of the people of God.

The great scandal of our modern times is the number of people who are leading congregations, but not spiritually qualified to do so. They read their Bibles only on Sunday when the preacher gives a text. Even then, it is a pew Bible and not their own. They spend more time fumbling with their television remote controls than they do reading their Bible and being empowered through God's Word. Although becoming biblical experts is unnecessary, leaders should know enough scripture to understand the importance and meaning of qualifying themselves spiritually to lead in God's church. How can people lead other people in a faith community, in a spiritual community, when they are of little faith and little spirit?

Developing a consistent devotional life helps the believer understand the importance of developing a strong spiritual life for service to Christ. Enhancing one's spiritual understanding helps one discover that help and strength rest not on oneself, but on Christ. It encourages the believer to know that his or her work in the church rests on a higher power and has larger implications than he our she could ever know.

Leaders can begin developing a devotional life through a piecemeal process of commitment. Begin formulating a pattern of weekly devotions by studying once a week and gradually over time build toward daily devotional study. If you have not cultivated the discipline of devotional study and practice, it is best to cultivate the discipline over a period of time. After a daily devotional time has been established, people discover its necessity in ongoing spiritual formation. The more leaders devote themselves to the study of God's Word through reading, meditation, and prayer, the stronger they become for spiritually leading God's church. A strong devotional life teaches discipline, patience, compassion, and under-standing—essential qualities of strong spiritual leaders.

It is crucial that leaders model the spirituality they profess and that they take seriously the imperatives for developing a strong devotional life for service.

Putting On and Keeping On the Full Armor of God: Doing Battle Against the Enemy God's Way

Paul exhorts us to put on the full armor of God (Eph. 6:10-18). We must not only put it on, but keep it on at all times. The paradox is that references to spiritual warfare are throughout the Bible, but Christians seem ill-prepared to fight the good fight. In fact, some of us are shocked at the nature and magnitude of warfare in the church. One wag stated that we must go through Old Testament wars to arrive at a New Testament faith. In my denomination, I seldom hear clergy talk of spiritual warfare and or even of the devil. Has the devil ceased to exist? Is evil a figment of the imagination? Too many Christians have ended up on the casualty list or missing in action, or ended up as spiritual prisoners of war because they were not prepared to fight the enemy. The enemy is not only others—the enemy is also us!

Conversely, those grounded in God's Word are seldom seduced into believing Christian spiritual warfare is a thing of the past. Some churches are well-acquainted with the importance of spiritual warfare training. They see the enemy wreaking havoc in the world and in the church. On the other hand, some liberal Protestant sem-inaries and churches have moved so far away from spir-itual basics that they have failed to train clergy and laity to fight the good fight or to think of ministry as actually doing battle against powers and principalities.

In some cases, church atrophy is nothing more than the devil taking control of the church. When people become hateful, obstinate, vicious, and malicious, as opposed to loving, just, caring, and joyful in their service to Christ, who and what is the influence here? Is it God or the devil?

In fighting the good fight we do not use the weapons of the world, but the weapons of God, says Paul (2 Cor. 10:1-6). The primary weapon is love. Fighting the way the world fights is fighting the devil's way, which undermines our spiritual authority. Sometimes to fight simply means nonviolent, noncooperation with evil. It means that evil will have neither your consent nor endorsement. This means doing things God's way as opposed to playing politics in the church.

Fighting the good fight means not repaying evil with evil. Paul gives a helpful reminder to Timothy in 2 Timothy 4:14-15. "Alexander the metalworker did me a great deal of harm. The Lord will repay him for what he has done. You too should be on your guard against him, because he strongly opposed our message." The Lord will repay. Fighting sometimes means having patience, endurance, and perseverance in the knowledge that God will have God's way. Repentance, forgiveness, and righteousness are also viable weapons, but nothing works better than love.

Christians should be spiritually trained to understand that the devil will show up, even in the church. But when the saints lose their sanity and composure every time this occurs, the spiritual training they have received comes into question. Good spiritual training teaches people how to handle situations when the devil appears. If people are truly grounded and living in the Word of God they will understand how problems can be solved, how people can be confronted in love, and how to create conditions of redemption rather than conditions of condemnation.

A Hungering for God's Word

Where is the genuine hungering for God's Word in our churches? Unfortunately, there appears to be a complacency in seeking God's Word in mainline Protestant denominations. It's almost as if seeking and thirsting for God's Word has gone out of style. What happened to our enthusiasm, hunger, and excitement for the Word of God? Have we become so stupefied in our modern culture, bombarded by words on the radio, billboards, newspapers, twenty-four-hour news stations, and advertising that we no longer have a desire to seek God's Word? We have been deluged by the "uniquack" of our larger culture.

The problem is we think we know all there is to know, that our modern secular education is enough to get us by and get us over. We think we know because we have been formally educated and trained and believe this will suffice as we fake our way through leading the church.

Many educated, middle-class persons believe that their formal training and education at a reputable university will suffice to qualify them as leaders in God's church. Nothing could be further from the truth. Formal training and education at a university may provide persons with certain gifts and skills for leadership in the church, but do not exclusively qualify one for leadership in God's church.

Numerous churches are impaired by such thinking. We cripple the church and hamper spiritual growth when we allow people to lead who are unprepared. *What is needed is a genuine hunger and thirst to study and learn God's Word, and a humility that will enable laypersons to submit to God's will as they seek to serve God's church.* If the church is to grow and be empowered spiritually, it must train Christians to be hearers, believers, and doers of God's Word.

Becoming Good Stewards of Time, Talent, and Treasure

God has blessed us with resources and appoints us to be good stewards over them. Sometimes in an effort to be good stewards we ruin our blessings and undermine the prosperity God has in store for us. Bishop Linda Lee has observed that money is too much of a problem in our churches.[1] African Americans have the eleventh largest income of any ethnic group in the world. Billions of dollars flow through our hands each year, but how are we harnessing and stewarding those resources? Unfortunately, we own little and manufacture virtually nothing. On average, a dollar turns over once in African American communities, but conversely, at least seven times in white communities. Moreover, a greater tragedy is how we have kept God's church hostage through poor stewardship. Although African American churches receive millions of dollars per week and several billions per year, where does it all go?

We must begin by teaching the stewardship of time, talent, and treasure—most preferably tithes—in the church. Too often churches use fund-raising gimmicks and programs that emphasize one-time giving rather than an ongoing financial commitment from parishioners. If every member tithed, that is gave 10 percent of their gross income to the church, congregations would likely not need another fund-raiser.

We must teach Christians the value of tithing and of making God's ministry a priority (Mal. 3:10). Too often tithing is viewed as a money matter, but the truth is it is also a spiritual matter. If the people of God set their spir-

itual priorities in place, then tithing becomes a manifestation of their spiritual commitment to Christ and the
church. At Hope Church we have established a Cheerful
Givers program, which allows members to move into
full tithing in three years. The first year they contribute
3 percent of their income, the second year they give 7
percent, and in the third year they become full-fledged
tithers by giving 10 percent of their gross income.
Moreover, the stewardship committee sponsors seminars that help parishioners learn more about the importance of tithing. Tithing is also taught in our new
members orientation classes, where new members are
introduced to biblical mandates for tithing.

In addition to being good stewards of our treasure, we
must also be mindful of our time and talent. Time is the
most precious resource we have because it is the only
thing we can give people and never get back. When we
give our time to something, we are valuing its importance. By giving our time to others we are saying they
are important to us. By giving our time to the church we
are affirming the church's importance in our lives.

Everyone has a talent or gift that is uniquely theirs
that they can offer in service to the church. A recurring
question posed to the members of Hope Church is *What
is the difference between Hope Church and all of the churches
in the history of Christianity?* "Me," they respond.

Each person can make a difference through the use of
his or her gift and by taking time for the glory of God.
God gives everyone talent, but the talent becomes a gift
when it is used for God's ministry. The gift is truly a gift
when used to inspire, encourage, and motivate others to
actualize their potential and serve Christ. Sometimes
people believe that if they give ample time and talent to
the church, they do not need to tithe. Although giving
time to the church is a good place to start, the ideal is to
have people donate their time, talent, and tithe to the

church. A member of Hope Church once excused himself from tithing because, as he said, "If my time were translated into money it would exceed 10 percent of the income I would give to the church as a tithe." I expressed my appreciation for his time because essentially he had a good point. However, I challenged, "Your time is an invaluable asset to this ministry. I am thankful for the time you give to this church. However, the truth is I cannot translate that into currency." God asks that we give time, talent, and tithe. Giving time is a blessing to the church, but we should all, as good stewards, strive to maximize our efforts in these three basic areas.

Encouraging members to be good stewards is an essential element of any empowerment ministry. Churches with dynamic empowerment ministries teach the importance of lay ownership and support of the church. In these churches the entire congregation is challenged to give their best in service to Christ, to set standards of excellence for the glory of God, and to put their stewardship where their faith is. If the church is to be empowered, we must take primary responsibility in practicing the principles of good stewardship. This means that people must discover, develop, and use their gifts in ministry by giving their time, talent, and tithes to ensure the church's future. The church is in need of *good* help, and every church that is truly empowered possesses a committed and caring community of believers who realize the importance of faithfully giving time, talent, and tithes to the ministry of Christ.

Can I Get a Witness?

Witnessing for Christ is not just for Jehovah's Witnesses. In fact, mainline denominations should study the evangelism efforts of Jehovah's Witnesses, which are not wholly incongruous with early Methodism.

Why are Christians afraid and ashamed to witness to others for Christ? Because of scriptural ignorance and illiteracy? Because they are shy? Because of false and grandiose notions of what it means to evangelize others? Because they are unaccustomed to witnessing to others? Every Christian who has a saving relationship with Jesus Christ should be ready to tell somebody what they have seen and heard through Christ. They should be ready to witness to someone else about God's amazing and saving grace.

However, in order to witness to others about God, one has to develop a testimony about what God has done in one's life. In order to testify about what God has done in our lives we have to give honor and glory to God, and develop a close personal relationship with God. *Many people don't want to witness for Christ because they don't know Christ! They don't have a bonafide, reified, saving relationship with Christ! They wouldn't know Christ if they saw him on the street!* Can I get a witness? Where are the witnesses? Why don't evangelism committees evangelize? Where are the witnesses for the Lord? What do mainline Protestant denominations do by way of grassroots, down-home, plain-people witnessing for Christ? Is that the stuff for the other folk? For the Holy Rollers and down-homers? How can we come to this point in our journey after all that God has done in our lives and not have a viable testimony for someone who needs Christ?

This is one of the great sins of our church. We have reached a point of stagnation, mediocrity, and complacency, and have lost the apostolic imperatives, the need for reaching and witnessing to others for Christ. Can I get a witness? Are such things beneath me now that I have arrived? What happened to our witness? To be in relationship with Christ means that we have to go and tell somebody what we have seen and heard and how we have been delivered by him!

Don't Run the Church, Serve the Church!

> Too often church leaders see themselves as elected to
> "run the church." In fact, leaders serve the congregation
> best when they see themselves in a mediating role. They
> mediate the gifts of others so everyone feels included.
> They mediate resources and authority to other groups
> and individuals so everyone has an opportunity to share
> his or her gifts.[2]

Because of a lack of training in the fundamentals of
Christian spiritual service and the culture of expectation
that is developed in each congregation, we sometimes
become prepossessed with running the church rather
than serving it. Too frequently church service becomes
an exercise in power politics where flexing our ecclesiastical muscles becomes more important than humbly sub-
mitting ourselves to God's authority and will for the
church.

The ministry of the church appears to be run more like
a business or government because the underlying principles of Christian spirituality are often absent. Part of
the problem may be attributed to calling the ministry
work areas instead of *service areas,* and *committees* rather
than *ministries.* Things seem more task than service oriented. There is the trustees committee instead of the
trustees ministry, and the finance committee rather than
the finance ministry. When we see ourselves serving on
committees rather than as being part of a larger ministry,
it is easy to get lost in the bureaucratic quagmires of
committee work and obviate the underlying spiritual
purposes for which those committees are called to do
God's service.

Although a church must observe the rules and precepts of good business and should be a good steward of
God's resources, it must remember that it is ultimately in

the business of calling people back to Christ, and in the business of helping people transform their lives and those of others through Christ. By allowing committees to become an end within themselves, churches can easily begin to engage in myopic power "politrics." Thus they become preoccupied with running the church like a business or corporation without considering that the church is first and foremost a ministry, called to preserve the gospel and to win souls to Christ.

Humility, honesty, and a desire to serve God's people will do much to negate the egotistical constraints that often bind churches into organizational religion rather than living spiritual ecclesia. Spiritual training and education are avenues that will help congregations clearly understand their purpose. Don't run the church. Serve the people and God will be pleased!

Summary Questions

1. As laity do you feel spiritually empowered to lead God's people in ministry?

2. What courses in spiritual training and development have you taken to qualify yourself for leadership in the church?

3. Do you have spiritual gifts for ministry? Do you utilize those gifts for God's glory in the church? How do you use your spiritual gifts in service? Have you taken a spiritual gifts inventory? Have your gifts been matched with specific ministries in the church?

4. Do you attend Bible study? Do you pray regularly? Do you have a consistent and regular devotional life? Are you in spiritual formation and development as preparation and strengthening for leadership in the church?

5. How do you handle conflict? Do you know what it means to put your spiritual armor on and to fight the good fight? Have you been trained in the basics of Christian spiritual warfare?

6. Can you recognize the enemy? Are you aware of the presence and reality of evil in the church and in yourself? How do you handle sin and the reality of evil in the church?

7. As leader in the church do you tithe? Are you a good steward of God's resources? How much time and talent have you or do you devote to the ministry of God's church? Do you understand the importance of tithing?

8. Are you a witness for Christ? Are you saved? Have you told others about God's working in your life? Have you witnessed to and brought others to Christ?

9. What is your basic attitude about service in the church? Are you interested in power or in serving? Do you encourage the participation of other laity in the mission and ministry of God's church? What is your basic leadership profile? Are you approachable, friendly, aloof, or distant?

10. Do you feel spiritually empowered to serve the church and its ministries? In other words, is it well with your soul?

11. List the programs or courses for Christian training in your church.

12. Are laity taught the meaning, value, and practice of Christian spirituality as a foundation for their leadership in the church?

13. Are laity taught how to be good practicing Christians and how to translate that practice into the life of the church? Explain.

14. Are all spiritual gifts recognized in your church? Are laity encouraged to discover and utilize their gifts for service in the church?

Summary Checklist

☐ Establish a lay academy for Christian training to teach the basics of Christian spirituality and how to live a Christian life.

☐ Establish a spiritual gifts ministry. Conduct a spiritual gifts inventory and evaluation.

☐ Enroll in Bible study and begin developing a consistent devotional life of prayer, devotion, and Bible study.

☐ Enroll in a course in spiritual warfare and learn how to put and keep your spiritual armor on and how to fight the good fight in the church's ministry and in the world.

☐ Begin developing a plan to give your time, talent, and tithes to the church, and offer courses that will empower you to be a good steward of God's resources.

☐ Establish a stewardship committee who will develop programs to empower the laity to be good stewards of their resources.

☐ Under the leadership of the clergy, Christian education, and the stewardship committee establish a Cheerful Givers and Tithers program to encourage the lay support of your ministry.

☐ Understand the difference and importance between serving the church in love and humility and running the church.

☐ Learn the importance of discipleship and witness as part of the church's ministry and mission. Enroll in courses that will enable you to become more effective disciples and witnesses for Christ.

CHAPTER FIVE

Truly Empowered: Reclaiming Our Evangelical and Spiritual Heritage

In order for churches to be effective and relevant, they must speak the cultural and spiritual language of the people in order to get their attention and reach them where they are. They must also possess a spiritual vitality and energy that quickens and convinces their souls to Christ. The mark of healthy churches is a wholesome and vital spirituality. Many mainline Protestant denominations in general, and United Methodism in particular, have forsaken their evangelical heritage in order to accommodate modern secular culture, and the perilous result has been a steady decline of those churches over the past twenty-five years.

Black and white churches of these mainline denominations are in great need of cultural relevancy and spiritual vitality. The problem has been that the black church, which has forsaken its African roots in order to identify with its larger white constituents, has thus alienated the black masses, whereas the white church has negated its evangelical roots in order to accommodate secular paganism and thus has become estranged from the white masses. Both black and white mainline churches have lost much of their spiritual fire and evangelical fervor. Much of this loss can be attributed to their accommodation to larger interests and the abandonment of those spiritual principles and cultural praxis that originally authenticated and empowered their movements in the early stages of their development.

The problem of United Methodism is particularly curious in light of the spiritual necrophilia plaguing present churches, where Word-centeredness, basic spiritual training and formation, evangelical outreach, spiritual gifting, witness, and the Wesleyan revival spirit are as foreign to these churches as oil is to water. This problem is particularly acute in light of Methodist history. How is it that Methodism could begin as a Holy Ghost revival movement, and has now become an institutional church so preoccupied with church structures that it has virtually sequestered and destroyed that spirit of vitality that once gave it life, power, and authority?

In many churches there is a spiritual lethargy, a ho-hum, matter-of-fact, business-as-usual approach to the gospel and Christian faith that gives it little power or distinction. How can churches be revitalized when the people have not had a genuine conversion experience, do not possess a revival spirit, and run the church rather than serve it? How can churches be revitalized when there is no joy for service, no power of conviction and Christian witness, and little or no celebration for a living and risen Christ? Why doesn't the church save souls—inviting people to Christ, stressing the importance of Bible study and Word-centeredness, developing a devotional life, and reaching others for Christ? Why is the church so defensive and apologetic about holiness, developing and cultivating spiritual gifts, and referencing and invoking the presence and power of the Holy Ghost in church life? Why are clergy and laity uncomfortable talking about the devil, fighting the good fight, and equipping themselves for spiritual warfare in our churches? Have we gotten so far away from foundational principles of the faith that we no longer have the power and authority to convince others for Christ?

We need to return to our evangelical heritage, to challenge the anti-intellectualism that has dampened the American evangelical movement and prompted certain intellectual defections from mainline Protestant denominations. Moreover, appropriating vital elements of the Wesleyan tradition and instituting basic spiritual training programs that will empower clergy and lay Christians to win souls to Christ and build God's kingdom are crucial for an empowered church.

It is imperative that we begin retrieving and celebrating the practices of our glorious past that influenced the formation of strong and viable congregations that are filled with the Holy Ghost; that we have experienced conversion, sanctification, and transformation; and are unwilling to apologize to the devil, secular culture, and the larger society for the faith and power we possess.

Churches will continue to decline, rot, and die if a change in outlook and spirit does not occur. We must not simply tinker with church structures and expect great change. We cannot simply do the same old things the same old way and expect to get new results. As Christians we must join together in a concerted effort to call the people back to God and to challenge them to grow in their witness and demonstration of God's Word for our time.

Whereas the cultural contexts and needs of black and white congregations may be different, we all suffer from the same or similar spiritual atrophy. Although we are different in many ways, we are also very similar. White and black churches are caught in the spin cycle of pagan culture and secular humanism. The time, then, for spiritual accommodation and apologetics are over.

There are still more unchurched people in America than churched, and yet churches are being closed. Organizations close, businesses close, social clubs close—but churches should never close! What does this say about the way we do church, about our practice of theology and our witness in the community? How can churches go out of the business of conducting God's business? Part of the answer is because we have stopped doing God's business God's way. We have failed to teach and retain those basic biblical, spiritual, and evangelical practices that bring favor from God and win souls to Christ. We have become so preoccupied that we have failed to serve, nurture, and cultivate the souls of people for service. We have become so secular in our approach to church life that we have lost our spiritual vitality.

The great tragedy is that we did not begin this way. The United Methodist Church, as well as other mainline denominations, began as a spirit-filled movement. If we are to regain our vitality, we must go back to those principles and practices that enabled the church to grow and prosper in its witness for Christ. These Wesleyan Methodist principles and practices of evangelical zeal gave impetus and power to several charismatic movements. Returning to the Bible and our history will help us remember who we are and whose we are, and open the door of revitalization for a glorious future.

Appendix A

Church Growth

I. Prevailing Myths, Assumptions, and Realities Preventing Church Growth in United Methodism*

1. United Methodists don't celebrate Christ in worship or church life.

2. United Methodist worship services are more contemplative than celebrative.

3. The average church size is 150 and therefore cannot grow much beyond this number.

4. Preaching is generally conversational and monotone.

5. Black United Methodist churches are more Anglocentric than Afrocentric.

6. United Methodists, as a rule, don't develop community-based ministries. They rely largely upon the global reach and missional objectives of the larger church.

7. United Methodist churches are more discipline-centered than Word-centered and Holy Spirit-Ghost filled.

8. Laity and clergy are often more concerned with *running* the church than with *serving* the church.

*Although this list is specific to The United Methodist Church, readers will find the information a helpful guide in identifying similar information about their own denominations.

9. Many churches do not have leadership training academies for laity. Leaders are not spiritually qualified to lead, are generally ignorant of the Bible, and do not have strong devotional lives, thus causing a crisis of leadership in the church.

10. Many churches live by stewardship excuses rather than by stewardship commitment. There is little focus on tithing, talents, and time.

11. Leadership is often rule-oriented rather than principle-centered.

12. Many churches spend more time tending to structures of the church than to meeting the real spiritual needs of people and ministering to them on the grounds of their ultimate concerns.

13. Many churches do not train laity in the gifts of the Holy Spirit and therefore the ministry does not bear fruit. (The churches that do train laity emphasize certain gifts over others.)

14. Churches are more interested in preserving the church edifice than saving souls for Christ.

15. Many churches do not have a written vision, a three- to five-year vision, or a strategic plan for growth.

16. Churches no longer disciple or evangelize the community for Christ in the Wesleyan tradition.

17. Churches no longer emphasize the anointing and movement in the Holy Spirit as an impetus for guidance and service.

18. Some churches are guided more by survival mentality than by biblical principles of hope, faith, miracles, and resting on God's promises.

19. Some churches are crippled by a what-it-costs approach to ministry rather than a what-it-pays approach to ministry.

20. Some churches live more by the seven last words, *we never did it that way before,* than by the seventeen most

important words, *there is no limit to what you can do if you don't mind who gets the credit.*

21. Some churches need to be converted to Christ because the direction and future of the church is determined by so-called power groups in the church rather than by Christ.

II. Why Churches Grow

1. Churches grow when they have a vision for the future.

2. Churches grow when they prioritize the study of God's Word as part of the personal and corporate life of congregations.

3. Churches grow when they are open to the leadership and guidance of the Holy Spirit.

4. Churches grow when they prioritize spiritual growth along with numerical growth.

5. Churches grow when they intentionally disciple others to Christ by evangelizing communities.

6. Churches grow when they continue to care and nurture God's people.

7. Churches grow through risk-taking, innovation, and stepping out on faith.

8. Churches grow when they corporately repent of their sins and look critically and constructively at themselves in order to grow and change.

9. Churches grow when they mobilize and nurture spiritual, human, and material resources for kingdom building.

10. Churches grow when a climate of healing, openness, hospitality, and positive change, where there is no fear of failure, is cultivated.

11. Churches grow when they develop relevant ministries and programs for empowerment and edification

that reach people on the grounds of their ultimate concerns.

12. Churches grow when they emphasize the anointing, the gifts of the Holy Spirit, and doing the Word of God.

III. Key Concerns

1. Discipling, saving souls, sustaining and nurturing souls, keeping souls in the church, teaching souls for Christ.

2. A trained laity and leadership who sees ministry as a life vocation rather than an avocation or hobby; laity who envision themselves as vital parts of a ministry and not simply as members of committees; laity and leadership who live Word-centered, spirit-filled, gift-manifesting lives for Christ.

3. Changing the thinking and spiritual orientation of members and congregations within mainstream denominations to be open to change.

4. Initiating back-to-basics programs in Bible literacy, evangelism, and membership care.

Appendix B

Vision Inventory

The following are basic steps that can be used to assess the vision for the church's future. Consider using the questions listed below in conjunction with *Vision 2000: Planning Ministry into the Next Century*, by Joe A. Harding and Ralph W. Mohney (Nashville: Discipleship Resources, 1991).

I. What Is My Current Image of the Church?

We have seen in the past ten years an explosion of literature suggesting ways to reenvision the church. The call for renewal has reverberated throughout the church. My firm belief is that this renewal must not only come from the "top down," but also from the "bottom up." In other words, much of the revitalization of the church will have to come from laity and local congregations as they dare to rethink and reconfigure the parameters of ministry for the future.

1. What is the predominant image shaping your current understanding of the church? Use adjectives to describe the church's mission, function, and purpose in the world.

2. What is the source of this current vision? What

things influenced the formation of your current under-standing of the church?

3. Which of these descriptions is the most salient image of the church in your mind?

4. What do you believe is the prevailing image of your church by the surrounding community and the people it serves?

In *Models of the Church*, Avery Dulles describes the church as "heralder of the good news, sacrament, mysti-cal communion, servant, and institution."[1] Other writers speak of church models as medieval, contemporary, and New Age. Perhaps your images are less formal. Many people use other terms to describe their image of the church: extended family; center of refuge; place of heal-ing; a problem-dumping ground; social club; business; community outreach or congregational inreach; a place for youth, the elderly, or families; training outpost; bureaucracy; cultural and spiritual center; hospitality center; celebration and praise center; rehabilitation cen-ter; empowerment center; teaching, reaching, preaching, and nurturing place.

5. Do your current descriptions of the church suffice in depicting your vision of the church? Explain.

6. What variances exist between your present image and the future vision of the church?

7. If disparities exist between your image of the church and what it should become, how will you recon-cile these various viewpoints? (These new images pro-vide the basis of your vision.)

8. How can you share and nurture these images with members of the congregation and community?

9. Are there members of your church who have similar images and visions?

10. Are there members of your church who do not share the same images?

11. In what ways can you share information with both of these groups that will help them see your vision and help you see theirs?

12. How can you and members hone a common vision from different images and perspectives?

II. How Can I Begin Reimaging My Vision of the Church?

- Take a word that you feel embodies the church's mission and personifies its future (you did this in the previous section). Now translate or envision programs and ministries in your church that make this word concrete. List the feelings, attitudes, or behaviors this word signifies for you and others. What images come to mind when this word is spoken and shared?

- Do these words energize, enervate, motivate, or dissipate? Can they inspire people to constructive action on behalf of the vision? Do they make you feel good? Do they create their own litany of participation? For example, if your paramount image of church is *love*, how can you see this word actualized in the church's ministry? How might love be actualized in programs or relationships that actualize your vision of the church?

The word *love* is the basis of the vision. It might be translated into programs ranging from assisting battered women who need love to establishing conflict resolution training for youth who don't love themselves and thus are always in conflict with others. Other words might be *caring, teaching, sharing, knowledge,* and so forth.

- Every vision has a series of descriptive words or adjectives constituting its foundation that can be translated into meaningful ministries. The question becomes *how do you get others to see and translate such ideas into meaningful ministries of the church?*

The process by which a vision is conceived, shared, developed, and implemented provides a blueprint for community-building in the church.

1. What image would you like to see your church become in the future? Why?

2. Who are the key players in the vision and what are their roles?

3. What needs, purposes, missions, descriptions, definitions, and objectives would your vision fulfill for you, the church, and the larger community?

4. What human, spiritual, and material resources are required to make the vision a reality? How will you galvanize them to make the vision happen?

5. How can you hone and share that vision so that others can see and buy into it?

6. What is a realistic time line for conceptualizing, sharing, developing, implementing, and evaluating the vision plan?

III. Basic Next Steps

1. Imagine, image, pray, and conceptualize a model of ministry for your church's future that will empower people for Christ and help the church realize its missional goals and objectives.

2. Conduct a survey of the congregation and community to determine their visions for the church. What grounds this vision? Why is this vision so important and relevant to their lives? How can you create a context or forum for sharing this vision long term?

3. Develop a list of words that describe your vision of the church, and list their translation possibilities for ministry in your present context.

4. Establish a Dream or Vision T.E.A.M.—*Together Everyone Achieves More*—of creative and innovative people to discuss and share your dreams for the church's ministry on a regular basis. This team will formulate a vision based upon input from a variety of people in the church and larger community.

5. Establish regular meeting times or vision dialogue with the church and community to nurture and cultivate these ideas into reality.

6. Develop a process for the formulation, clarification, dissemination, and evaluation of the vision.

7. Establish time lines for vision implementation. Write the vision plan and share it with the congregation.

8. Implement the vision plan.

9. Translate you dream or vision ideas into possible practical programs that will help the church personify your vision.

- What are these programs?
- How can they be developed?
- Who will most benefit from them?
- How, when, and where can you translate and implement these visions into viable programs for the church's future?
- Who will sustain them?
- How will they be perpetuated?
- What processes of evaluation will be developed to test the vision's feasibility?

10. How much time is needed to establish the vision plan? Why is this time line more feasible than others?

11. Does the vision communicate and celebrate the people of Christ? Does the vision articulate and propagate the mission of the church? Does the vision say all we want it to say about who Christ is in the life of the church?

12. Make sure your visions are connected to the real needs of people in your church and the larger community.

13. Find ways of sharing the vision and encouraging people to buy into it for the long haul. Write your vision plan and share it with the church.

14. Have the courage to conceive and innovate for future possibilities.

15. Trust God, have faith, and pray.

16. Look to the Bible and contemporary experiences for examples of visionary leadership.

Appendix C
Christian Training
Academy Curriculum
(The following is a sampling of courses
offered through a Christian Training Academy.)

New Leader Track

Description   The New Leader is primarily for new ministry work area leaders who have either never been church leaders before or have not been church leaders at Hope United Methodist Church. It provides training on leadership styles, compares leadership processes of today to those used in the Bible, and describes the skills necessary to be an effective leader.

Current and previous leaders are also encouraged to take any of the courses in this track.

Course	Description	Hours	Possible Resources
Spiritual Leadership	Describes Christian leadership skills required to effectively lead teams of people in the church.	4	• *Spiritual Leadership* • *Jesus Christ, CEO* • *The Holy Bible*
Team Building	Demonstrates how to get a ministry work area to work together to set and achieve goals.	4	• *Jesus Christ, CEO* • *The Holy Bible*
Establishing and Managing the Ministry Work Area Budget	Guidelines for determining what a ministry work area's financial needs are, requesting and processing funds, and maintaining financial records.	2-4	

Course	Description	Hours	Possible Resources
Policies and Procedures Workshop	Provides instruction and guidelines for writing, updating, and maintaining policies and procedures for Hope United Methodist Church's ministry work area.	2	
Effective Meeting Techniques	Defines how to establish an agenda, define and implement consensus decision making, start/end a meeting.	4	
Christian Conflict Resolution Committee Leaders	Defines how church leaders can effectively resolve committee conflicts.	4	• *The Holy Bible*
Leadership Styles	Defines the various leadership styles and leadership responsibilities as they relate to the church.	4	• *The Holy Bible* • *Jesus Christ, CEO*
Effective Use of Volunteers	Defines how to utilize ministry work area members.	4	• *Empowering Lay Volunteers* • *How to Mobilize Church Volunteers*

Course	Description	Hours	Possible Resources
How to Study the Bible	Gives basic instruction on Bible reading.	8	• *The Holy Bible* • *Other resources*
How to Develop an Active Prayer Life	Teaches persons how to develop prayer life and how to pray.	8	• *The Holy Bible* • *Other resources*
Becoming Good Stewards of God's Resources	Teaches persons how to become effective stewards through tithing, time, and talents.	8	• *Various resources*
How to Develop a Devotional Life	Teaches fundamentals of daily devotion.	4	• *The Holy Bible* • *Other resources*
Church Leadership and the Holy Spirit	Teaches importance of Holy Spirit in serving the church.	8	• *The Holy Bible* • *Other resources*
Developing Your Spiritual Gifts	Teaches how to recognize and use spiritual gifts in ministry.	8	• *The Holy Bible* • *Other resources*

Christian Training Academy Curriculum

Current and Previous Leader Track

Description   This track is for current or previous ministry work area leaders who wish to enhance their skills. These leaders may also take any of the courses from the New Leaders and Ministry Work Area Members tracks.

Course	Description	Hours	Possible Resources
State of the Church Address/ Ministry Work Area Orientation	Presents pastor's annual State of the Church Address and Ministry Work Area Orientation in which the work areas are charged with goals and objectives for the year.	4	• *Pastor's Vision Plan*
The Interconnectional Church	Introduces the history and structure of both The United Methodist Church and Hope United Methodist Church. Hope's ministry work area structure will be presented during this seminar.	4	• *The Book of Discipline* • *The Book of Resolutions* • *Multiply God's Love*
Prayer and the Church Leadership	Defines the role prayer plays in leadership.	4	• *Spiritual Leadership* • *The Holy Bible*

Course	Description	Hours	Possible Resources
Leadership Symposium	Provides a 1½ day retreat with all of the leadership from Hope United Methodist Church in which strategic plans for the ministry work areas are presented. Each ministry work area compiles new budget and policies for the upcoming year in alignment with the Pastor's Vision Plan.	12	• *Pastor's Vision Plan*
Time and Project Management	Introduces time and project management skills for organizing and directing ministry work area projects.	4	
Increasing Leadership Effectiveness	Introduces new tools that will increase the effectiveness of the leaders.	4	• *Building God's People: A Workbook for Empowering Servant Leaders*
Recruiting New Ministry Work Area Leaders	Defines how to effectively bring new members into a ministry work area.	4	• *The Vital Congregation*

Course	Description	Hours	Possible Resources
Mentoring New Leaders	Describes how to prepare the next leader of a work area to assume the leadership role.	4	
Spiritual Warfare	How to do spiritual battle God's way.	8	• *Spiritual Warfare* • *Possessing the Gates of the Enemy* • *The Holy Bible*

Christian Training Academy Curriculum

Ministry Work Area Member Track

Description   The Ministry Work Area Member Track is for people who are interested in working on a ministry work area. It provides them with a foundation of information about The United Methodist Church structure, Hope United Methodist Church, the spiritual path, their spiritual gifts, and the pastor's vision for the church.

All leaders are welcome to take any of these courses.

Course	Description	Hours	Possible Resources
State of the Church Address/ Ministry Work Area Orientation	Presents pastor's annual State of the Church Address and Ministry Work Area Orientation in which the work areas are charged with goals and objectives for the year.	4	• *Pastor's Vision Plan*
The Interconnectional Church	Introduces the history and structure of both The United Methodist Church and Hope United Methodist Church. Hope's ministry work area structure will be presented during this seminar.	4	• *The Book of Discipline* • *The Book of Resolutions* • *Multiply God's Love*

Course	Description	Hours	Possible Resources
The Journey	Defines what it means to be a Christian and how to serve the Lord through volunteer work in the church.	16	• *The Believer's Handbook* • *Discover Your God-given Gifts* • *Your Spiritual Gifts*
Spiritual Gifts	Assists participation in discovering God-given spiritual gifts and teaches how to use those gifts for God's glory in the church.	4	• *Discover Your God-given Gifts* • *Your Spiritual Gifts*
How to Study the Bible	Gives basic instruction on Bible reading.	8	• *The Holy Bible* • *Other resources*
How to Develop an Active Prayer Life	Teaches persons how to develop prayer life and how to pray.	8	• *The Holy Bible* • *Other resources*
Becoming Good Stewards of God's Resources	Teaches persons how to become effective stewards through tithing, time, and talents.	8	• *Various resources*

Christian Training Academy Curriculum

Description   There are special skills and knowledge necessary to fully function as a guardian over the children at Hope United Methodist Church. In Jesus Junction, the ROCK, and our nursery, we serve more than the children of Hope, but their friends and family members as well. Therefore, we must prepare ourselves for the safety and safekeeping of our children through God's word, our time, talent, and gifts. The courses below are designed to support the guardianship you have accepted as a member of any children's ministry at Hope. The following are electives to the course requirements for certification by the Christian Training Academy.

Code	Course Title	Prerequisite	Hours	Course Description
CMH 095	Role Models for Children	None	3	An awareness course on body language and habits that children may model based on learned behavior.
REG 099	Child Registration	None	TBD	Registration procedure and software training to enroll children participants and their parents/guardians at HUMC.

Code	Course Title	Prerequisite	Hours	Course Description
VOL 100	Volunteerism	None	3	An introduction to volunteerism at Hope UMC. This course provides an overview of the pastor's vision, the ministry model, the levels of ministries in the church, and training for certification to serve at these levels.
CMH 100	Volunteering with Children of Special Needs	VOL 100	3	This course reviews special needs of children and how to minister to them. Focus is on the emotionally challenged.
CMH 101	Child Education (Ages 5-12)	None	TBD	Introductory course on how children learn (ages 5-12).
CMH 102	Child Education (Ages 13-18)	CMH 101	TBD	Introductory course on how children learn (ages 13-18).
CMH 103	Children and Christian Faith	CMH 101	TBD	Instruction on how children experience Christ, the commit-ment of the church to children, and policies and attitudes affecting children. This course is designed for child advocates, program directors, teachers, pastors, and parents.

Code	Course Title	Prerequisite	Hours	Course Description
CMH 104	Teaching Creativity	CMH 103	3	Teaching creativity in children.
CMH 200	First Aid and CPR	None	3	Basic training in emergency first aid to children and adults while on church premises.
CMH 201	Child Health Care 201	CMH 200	TBD	A course to instruct in proper sanitation and disease control while working with food and children.
CMH 202	Child Protection Acts	None	TBD	An overview of federal and State of Michigan statutes governing the care and welfare of children.
CMH 301	Child Discipline 101	None	TBD	Correcting behavior in children.
CMH 302	Child Discipline 102	CMH 101, CMH 102	TBD	Correcting behavior in children.
CMH 303	Church Public Safety 101	CMH 200, CMH 201, and CMH 202	TBD	A course in the safety of children while on the church premises. Provides information on federal and State of Michigan child protection, law enforcement, the Hope Church incident reporting procedure, and registration of children.

Notes

Introduction

1. Paulo Freire, *Pedagogy of the Oppressed* (New York: Seabury Press, 1970), 56.

2. Toward a Model of Spiritual Empowerment

1. Rick Warren, *The Purpose Driven Church* (Grand Rapids, Mich.: Zondervan Publishing House, 1995), 85-94.

2. Edmund Robb, "Why Is the United Methodist Church Declining?" *The Challenge to Evangelism Today* 20, no. 1 (summer 1987): 1.

3. Richard Hofstadter, *Anti-Intellectualism in American Life* (New York: Random House, 1963), 55-116.

4. See Albert Outler, *Evangelism in the Wesleyan Spirit* (Nashville: Tidings Press, 1971).

5. Mark A. Noll, *The Scandal of the Evangelical Mind* (Grand Rapids, Mich.: Eerdmans, 1994), 3-42.

6. Ibid., 43-56. I am using this term to refer to all persons belonging to mainline Protestant denominations, which include: United Methodist, Episcopalian, Presbyterian, Lutheran, American Baptist, and others.

7. Conversations with parishioners at Hope United Methodist Church, Southfield, Mich., February 1986.

8. Conversations with a United Methodist pastor, May 1999.

9. Albert Outler, *Evangelism in the Wesleyan Spirit*, 53.

10. Albert Outler, ed., *John Wesley* (New York: Oxford University Press, 1964), 66.

11. Richard Wilke, *And Are We Yet Alive?* (Nashville: Abingdon Press, 1988), 29.

12. Ibid., 34.

13. James C. Logan, "The Evangelical Imperative: A Wesleyan

Perspective," in *Theology and Evangelism in the Wesleyan Heritage*, ed. James C. Logan (Nashville: Kingswood Press, 1994), 15.

14. Carlyle Fielding Stewart III, "Holiness, Black Methodism, and the Wesleyan Evangelical Tradition: Prospects for Revitalizing the Black United Methodist Church," Methodist Lectures, Garrett-Evangelical Theological Seminary, Evanston, Ill., April 9, 1996.

15. George G. Hunter III, *To Spread the Power: Church Growth in the Wesleyan Spirit* (Nashville: Abingdon Press, 1987), 53-56.

16. Daniel Buttry, *Bringing Your Church Back to Life: Beyond Survival Mentality* (Valley Forge, Penn.: Judson Press, 1988), 67.

17. Manfred Marquardt, *John Wesley's Social Ethics: Praxis and Principles* (Nashville: Abingdon Press, 1952), 27-29.

18. Donald W. Dayton, *Theological Roots of Pentecostalism* (Peabody, Mass.: Hendrickson Publishers, 1987), 35-60. See also Donald W. Dayton's *Discovering an Evangelical Heritage* (Peabody, Mass.: Hendrickson Publishers, 1976).

19. Robert W. Rae, "Strengthen Your Faith" in *The Upper Room* 60, no. 2 (May-June 1994): 30.

3. Clergy Empowerment

1. Craig R. Hickman, *Mind of a Manager, Soul of a Leader* (New York: John Wiley & Sons, 1990), 1-18.

2. Conversations with Rev. Dr. Philip Harley at Southlawn United Methodist Church, June 1997.

3. See Joe A. Harding and Ralph W. Mohney's *Vision 2000: Planning for Ministry into the Next Century* (Nashville: Discipleship Resources, 1991).

4. Lay Empowerment

1. Conversations with Dr. Linda Lee, Hope United Methodist Church, Southfield, Mich., 1999.

2. Thomas R. Hawkins, *Building God's People: A Workbook for Empowering Servant Leaders* (Nashville: Discipleship Resources, 1990), 63.

Appendix B

1. Avery Dulles, *Models of the Church* (Garden City, N.Y.: Doubleday, 1974)

Bibliography

Anders, Max. *What You Need to Know About Spiritual Warfare.* Nashville: Thomas Nelson, 1997.

Armstrong, John H., ed. *The Coming Evangelical Crisis.* Chicago: Moody Press, 1996.

Baldwin, Lewis V. "Early African American Methodism." In *Heritage and Hope: The African American Presence in United Methodism.* Nashville: Abingdon Press, 1991.

Barna, George. *The Index of Leading Spiritual Indicators.* Waco: Word Publishing, 1996.

_____. *Evangelism that Works.* Ventura, Calif.: Regal Books, 1995.

Blackaby, Henry T., and Claude V. King. *Fresh Encounter: Experiencing God in Revival and Spiritual Awakening.* Nashville: Broadman & Holman, 1996.

Braaten, Carl E. *The Apostolic Imperative.* Minneapolis: Augsburg Press, 1985.

Brawley, James P. *Two Centuries of Methodist Concern.* New York: Vantage Press, 1974.

Buttry, Daniel. *Beyond Survival Mentality.* Valley Forge, Pa.: Judson Press, 1988.

Callahan, Kennon L. *Giving and Stewardship in an Effective Church.* San Francisco: HarperSanFranscisco, 1992.

Churruarin, Juan Jose. *The Lost of the Anointing.* Kent, U.K.: Sovereign World Press, 1995.

Conger, Jay A. *The Charismatic Leader.* San Francisco: Josey-Bass, 1992.

Costen, Melva Wilson. *African American Christian Worship.* Nashville: Abingdon Press, 1993.

Cox, Harvey. *Fire From Heaven: The Rise of Pentecostal Spirituality and the Reshaping of Religion in the Twenty-first Century.* New York: Addison-Wesley, 1995.

Cueni, Robert R. *The Vital Church Leader.* Nashville: Abingdon Press, 1991.

Dayton, Donald W. *Discovering an Evangelical Heritage.* Peabody, Mass.: Hendrickson Publishers, 1976.

_____. *Theological Roots of Pentecostalism.* Peabody, Mass.: Hendrickson Publishers, 1987.

Flynn, Leslie B. *19 Gifts of the Spirit.* Eastbourne, U.K.: Chariot Victor Publishing, 1974.

Fortune, Don and Katie. *Discover Your God-given Gifts.* Grand Rapids: Chosen Books, 1999.

Freire, Paulo. *Pedagogy of the Oppressed.* New York: Seabury Press, 1970.

Greenleaf, Robert K. *Servant Leadership.* New York: Paulist Press, 1977.

Haddal, Ingvar. *John Wesley.* Nashville: Abingdon Press, 1961.

Harding, Joe A., and Ralph W. Mohny. *Vision 2000: Planning for Ministry into the Next Century.* Nashville: Discipleship Resources, 1991.

Harper, Steve. *John Wesley's Message for Today.* Grand Rapids: Zondervan, 1983.

Hawkins, Thomas R. *Building God's People.* Nashville: Discipleship Resources, 1990.

Heitzenrater, Richard P. *The Elusive Mr. Wesley.* Vols. 1 and 2. Nashville: Abingdon, 1984.

_____. *Wesley and the People Called Methodists.* Nashville: Abingdon Press, 1995.

Heitzenrater, Richard P., and Frank Baker, eds. *The Bicentennial Edition of the Works of John Wesley.* Nashville: Abingdon Press, 1995.

Hickman, Craig. *Mind of a Manager, Soul of a Leader.* New York: John Wiley & Sons, 1990.

Hofstadter, Richard. *Anti-Intellectualism in American Life.* New York: Random House, 1963.

Hunter, George G., III. *To Spread the Power: Church Growth in the Wesleyan Spirit.* Nashville: Abingdon Press, 1987.

Johnston, Hank, and Bert Klandermans, eds. *Social Movements and Culture.* Minneapolis: University of Minneapolis Press, 1995.

Jones, Ezra Earl. *Quest for Quality in the Church.* Nashville: Discipleship Resources, 1993.

Klaas, Alan C. *In Search of the Unchurched.* Bethesda: The Alban Institute, 1996.

Klaiber, Walter. *Call and Response Biblical Foundation of a Theology of Evangelism.* Nashville: Abingdon Press, 1997.

Kraft, Charles H., and Mark White, eds. *Behind Enemy Lines.* Ann Arbor: Servant Publications, 1994.

Linn, Jan G. *What Ministers Wish Church Members Knew.* St. Louis: Chalice Press, 1995.

Logan, James C., ed. *Theology and Evangelism in the Wesleyan Heritage.* Nashville: Kingswood Books, 1994.

McClain, William B. *Black People in the Methodist Church*. Nashville: Abingdon Press, 1984.

McMakin, Jacqueline, and Rhoda Nary. *Discovering Your Gifts, Vision, and Call*. San Francisco: HarperSanFrancisco, 1993.

Malina, Bruce J. *The Social World of Jesus*. London: Routledge Press, 1996.

Marquardt, Manfred. *John Wesley's Social Ethics*. Nashville: Abingdon Press, 1992.

Miller, Herb. *The Vital Congregation*. Nashville: Abingdon Press, 1990.

Nanus, Burt. *Visionary Leadership*. San Francisco: Josey-Bass, 1992.

Nichols, Roy C. *Doing the Gospel*. Nashville: Abingdon Press, 1990.

Noll, Mark A. *The Scandal of the Evangelical Mind*. Grand Rapids: Eerdmans, 1994.

Norwood, Frederick A. *The Story of American Methodism*. Nashville: Abingdon Press, 1974.

Oden, Thomas C., Leicester R. and Longden, eds. *The Wesleyan Theological Heritage Essays of Albert Outler*. Grand Rapids: Zondervan, 1991.

O'Murchu, Diarmuid. *Reclaiming Spirituality*. New York: Crossroads Publishers, 1998.

Outler, Albert. *Evangelism in the Wesleyan Spirit*. Nashville: Tidings Press, 1971.

Outler, Albert, ed. *John Wesley*. New York: Oxford University Press, 1964.

Page, Sidney H. T. *Powers of Evil*. Grand Rapids: Baker Books, 1995.

Rediger, Lloyd. *Clergy Killers*. Louisville: Westminster John Knox Press, 1997.

Reid, Frank Madison. *The Nehemiah Plan*. Shippensburg, Pa.: Destiny Image, 1994.

Richey, Russell E.; Kenneth E. Rowe; and Jean Miller Schmidt. *Perspectives on American Methodism*. Nashville: Kingswood Books, 1993.

Rusbulolt, Richard E. *A Workbook on Biblical Stewardship*. Grand Rapids: Eerdmans, 1994.

Sanders, J. Oswald. *Spiritual Leadership*. Chicago: Moody Press, 1980.

Schaller, Lyle E. *44 Ways to Increase Church Attendance*. Nashville: Abingdon Press, 1988.

Sherrer, Quin, and Ruthanne Garlock. *The Spiritual Warrior's Prayer Guide*. Ann Arbor: Servant Publications, 1992.

Stewart, Carlyle Fielding, III. *African American Church Growth*. Nashville: Abingdon Press, 1994.

_____. "Holiness, Black Methodism, and the Wesleyan Evangelical Tradition: Prospects for Revitalizing the Black United Methodist Church." Methodist Lectures, Garrett-Evangelical Theological Seminary, April 9, 1996, Evanston, Ill.

Stokes, Mack B. *The Bible in the Wesleyan Heritage*. Nashville: Abingdon Press, 1979.

Stringfellow, William. *The Politics of Spirituality*. Philadelphia: Westminster Press, 1984.

Tabraham, Barrie. *The Making of Methodism*. London: Epworth Press, 1995.

Tillich, Paul, *Systematic Theology*. Vol. 1. Chicago: University of Chicago Press, 1951.

Tippit, Sammy. *The Choice America at the Crossroads of Ruin and Revival*. Chicago: Moody Press, 1998.

Wagner, Peter. *The Healthy Church*. Ventura: Calif.: Regal Books, 1996.

Warren, Rick. *The Purpose Driven Church*. Grand Rapids: Zondervan, 1995.

White, Woodie, ed. *Our Time Under God Is Now*. Nashville: Abingdon Press, 1993.